THE STORY OF RO

Phoebe Berrow, Barbara Burbridge and Pat Genge

The Story of ROMSEY

FIRST PUBLISHED 1984

Reprinted 1993

LTVAS GROUP
3 Linden Road, Romsey, Hampshire

ISBN 0 906921 06 6

Printed in Great Britain by
Borcombe Printers plc, Romsey, Hampshire

Contents

Cover illustration
The Market Place, early 20th century. Sunday Schools Procession – before walking to Whitnap or Broadlands for the Sunday School Treat.

Preface

This is only a short book and Romsey has a very long history. We ask our readers to forgive the omissions they undoubtedly notice.
The twelve years' work of the LTVAS Group has produced a vast quantity of fascinating historical material, as well as hints and leads to information yet uncovered.

Phoebe Berrow
Barbara Burbridge
Pat Genge

March 1984

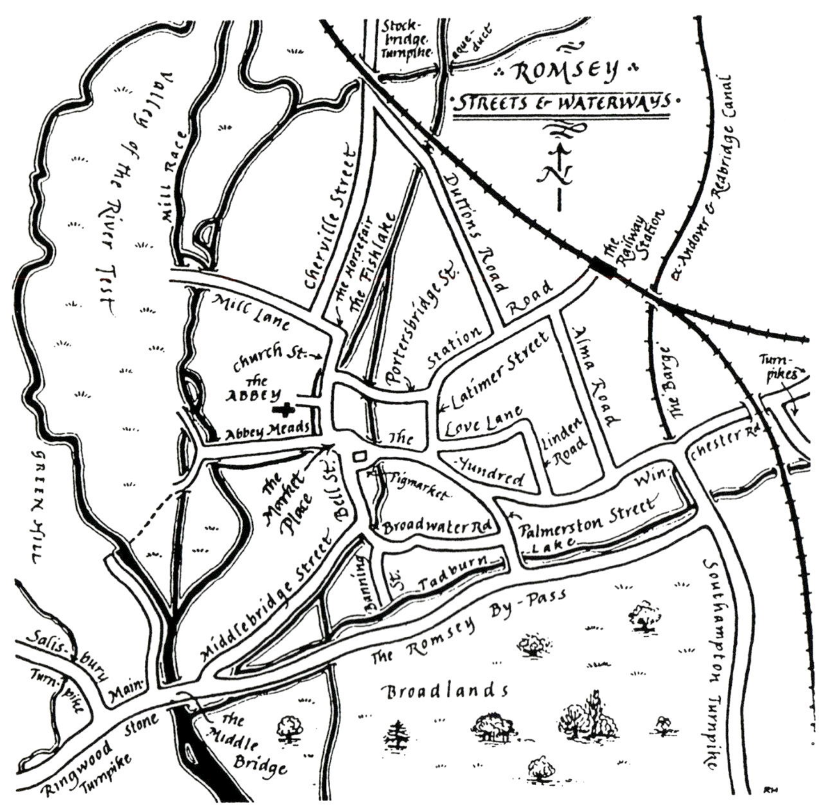

Romsey in the past was known as "Romsey in the mud". A study of the waterways will show the reason for the title.

Out of the Marshes

Romsey is a small town, well known for its Abbey and Broadlands, the stately home associated with Lord Mountbatten. However, great abbeys and stately homes do not exist in isolation and between and around these two is the town of Romsey. Its buildings do not fill the pages of coffee table books about architecture but it has a beguiling charm that springs from the homely scale of its narrow streets and modest buildings.

The Abbey church is several centuries older than Broadlands. It was in Saxon times that a religious house was founded, built on a gravel platform in the flood plain of the River Test, which flows to the west of the town. The present Abbey church is a Norman building, squat and substantial, on the edge of Romsey. From the top of Green Hill (the A27 road to Salisbury), it can be seen surrounded by trees and fields separated from the hill by the river, as it winds through the meadows of its lower reaches.

The town has grown from obscure beginnings but was a flourishing settlement by the time of the Norman Conquest. The core of Romsey is the triangular-shaped market place, similar to those found in other market towns stimulated by the presence of a monastery or castle. The prime trading positions would have been under the protective shadow of the Abbey wall, funnelling down into an elongated triangle as the less favoured traders pushed forward to attract customers.

The Test rises in the chalk lands of Ashe between Andover and Basingstoke. It works its way west and south between the downs of northern Hampshire to the broad valley in which Romsey is situated. It is one of the two main rivers that flow into Southampton Water, that inlet of the sea north of the Isle of Wight. The other river is the Itchen which rises in central Hampshire and flows through Winchester to eastern Southampton. The Test reaches Southampton on the western side, and today it forms part of the Western Docks which accommodate some of the world's largest ships. A little further north, as it skirts to the east of the Totton area, it remains tidal and rather barren, its banks a mass of rushes and mudflats. The enthusiastic fresh-water fisherman would be hard put to recognise any relationship with the renowned salmon and trout stream which is revered the world over. Some miles upstream, however, the Test is true to its famed character; a fast moving flow of rippling silver water with, in modern times, attractive banks, now open and grassy and now tree shaded. At Romsey it presents a most fascinating complexity.

Romsey from Greenhill. The Abbey still dominates the town when seen from the Salisbury Road, as it has done for many centuries.

Like rivers everywhere it has shaped its own environment. When the sea level was low, the river flowed swiftly and carved through the gentle hills. When the ice caps melted and the sea levels rose the water moved slowly and dropped its load, forming gravel terraces along the way. It is on one such terrace that people settled and which is now the heart of old Romsey.

The early settlers must have lived very much on an island in the mud. To this day the whole area is laced with streams and it is only by man's drainage, road and bridge building skills that the valley is passable in wet weather. Our early ancestors, lacking our technology, would have had to find other ways of coping with their environment.

The gravels around Romsey have yielded a variety of fossils and flint implements over the years, some of which have been washed downstream but others clearly indicate local settlement. The hill forts of the surrounding chalk lands are well known, such as the earthworks of Badbury Rings, Old Sarum, Danebury and St. Catherine's Hill. The valley floor settlements leave much less trace, even to the skilled archaeologist. The network of streams and the marshy ground would have constituted a different form of defence. The river would have been a source of food (fish), of plentiful water, which was always in short supply on hill forts, and the valley land was suitable for grazing herds or cereal growing. It could also have been a transport artery.

There are distinct signs of occupation of the Romsey area from 1000 B.C. The people of that time seem to have come here seasonally and it was not until about 500 B.C. that permanent settlement occurred, which is late compared with settlements on higher ground. Bronze Age axes have been found at Wellow, to the west, a Bronze Age torque, (or necklace and pin) at Jermyn's Lane to the east, and pottery in the town centre. To the south of Romsey at Skidmore, a gold torque was found, from the Iron Age. There was a Romano-British settlement in Romsey but present discoveries do not suggest it was of such importance as the Palace of Fishbourne, Roman Winchester or Clausentum in Southampton. However, monumental stones of Roman date have been incorporated into the fabric of the Abbey church and Roman glass and hoards of coins have been found on the outskirts of Romsey. One coin, found in central Romsey, was minted as far away as the land now called Yugoslavia. Roman Romsey may have been an unspectacular farming community but there were impressive villas nearby at Braishfield, Ampfield, Sparsholt and West Dean.

The Old English "ey" means "island", and it is often suggested that the name Romsey means "Roman's Island". If this interpretation of the name is correct, it could indicate that the later Saxon Romsonians had either tangible and recognisable Roman remains, or that it was remembered in the folklore of the district. Tradition attributes the Fishlake stream to Roman builders and this artificial water channel divides from the main River Test north of the town. The Fishlake marked the ancient boundary between Romsey Infra and Romsey Extra, before joining the tributary stream known as the Tadburn, which flows into the Test to the south of the town.

The earliest English settlers here entered Hampshire in the fourth century as Roman mercenaries. When Roman Britain declined and broke into small units, it seems that more mercenaries were brought in and they gradually took over from their departing masters. They avoided the Roman sites and settled on the hidden wastelands. So far there is no evidence of continuous settlement to connect Roman and Saxon Romsey.

Excavations have revealed eighth century iron-smelting and pottery as the earliest signs of Saxon habitation. By this time there was probably some form of religious settlement, although the formal monastic establishment appears to be later.

By the tenth century certainly, a major monastery of nuns had been established in Romsey, who lived and worshipped on the site of the present Abbey church. In 967, King Edgar granted the nuns large tracts of land in Romsey, and again the rivers and streams formed the boundaries, notably the Test on the west, the "Fareburne" to the north, and others to the east.

The easiest part of the land boundary to see is the Bishop's Mark or Bank, which crosses the Straight Mile at Ampfield. This bank was built by a Saxon Bishop of Winchester to mark the limits of his woodland.

Romsey is only twelve miles from Winchester and lies between that city and the New Forest. The Saxon and Norman kings used to hunt in the Forest and Romsey formed a convenient staging post. It is also near a convenient crossing point of the river, now called Middlebridge, and this acted as a focus for travellers. What was more natural then for the tenth century King Edgar to reform and revitalise the monastery at Romsey as part of his programme of monastic reform? His patronage, and the proximity to Winchester, helped the Abbey to be rich and fashionable.

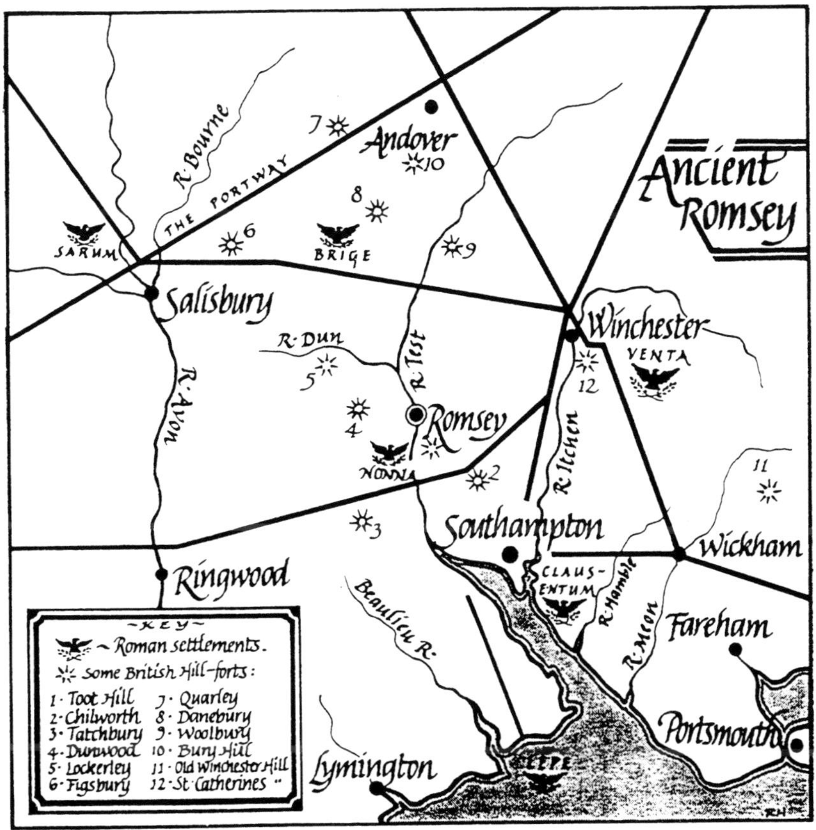

The ancient trackways and roads, the hill forts and Roman settlements indicate that this part of Hampshire has been inhabited for thousands of years.

The ladies who came to be Benedictine nuns at Romsey, were from the greatest families in the land. Other great ladies stayed here as paying guests, and many young ladies grew up under the care of the nuns in their school. King Alfred's granddaughter Aelflaeda was a tenth century Abbess. Christina, one of the last Saxon princesses, was Abbess in the eleventh century and her niece Matilda grew up in her care, partly at Romsey and partly at the nunnery at Wilton. Matilda married Henry I, the son of William the Conqueror in 1100, thus uniting Saxon and Norman royal families and removing a political threat to the Norman rulers.

The presence of all these wealthy people was a great stimulus to trade. There were about a hundred nuns at this time, and their pupils and guests added to the numbers. They would have had servants, and all these people needed housing, clothing and feeding. The Abbey must have been almost a permanent building site, providing much work erecting and maintaining domestic accommodation as well as the church. The remains of a large Saxon church can still be seen through a trap door in the north transept of the present, Norman, church. As well as producing a large demand for supplies, the Abbey established a weekly market in the town and organised two trade fairs a year. This patronage brought more trade to the area and would have helped the growth and the importance of Romsey.

Romsey as described in the Domesday Book of 1086.

The Medieval Abbey and Town

The five centuries that followed the Norman Conquest saw the Abbey's years of glory, its decline and its end, swept away by Henry VIII when he dissolved the monasteries of England. The town, made prosperous by the great Abbey, grew and flourished; Romsey took advantage of the changing balance in farming. A gradual move to sheep farming, accelerated by the Black Death plagues of the 1340s heightened the industrial development of the Middle Ages. England became wealthy by selling first wool, and then woollen cloth, and merchants in Romsey gained financial independence of their protector. By the time the Abbey was dissolved in 1539, the town had a community of affluent merchants, tanners and yeomen who were able to take over the running of civic affairs.

The first glimpse of individual Romsonians is given in the Domesday Book of 1086. Twenty years after conquering England, William I decided to take stock of the country and ordered a survey of all the land holders and their holdings. The results were collated and written down in the Domesday Book, which can still be seen in the Public Record Office in London. The entry for Romsey showed that about a hundred people held land in the immediate area. Those land holders would have had households of their own and together with the nuns and their servants, this would imply a population of several hundreds.

The town of Romsey and the land on the east of the Test were mostly held by the Abbess. Other lands in what is now the rural part of Romsey were held by other people. The most prominent of them was Bernard Pancevolt, who was one of the Norman followers of William I. William had rewarded many of his army with gifts of English lands and he had given the areas now known as Pauncefoot Hill and Embley to Bernard. The Pancevolt (or Pauncefoot) family kept those lands for over four hundred years until Peter Pauncefoot, the last male heir, died at the age of nine in 1493. Their name is preserved in the hill that brings the traveller into Romsey from the direction of the New Forest. The Pauncefoots do not seem to have lived in Romsey nor to have played a great part in its affairs, although some ladies from the family joined the Abbey as nuns.

As principal land holder, the Abbess was the major ruler of Romsey. Within the town itself, she, through her steward, controlled the day-to-day life of the town and dealt with most lawbreaking. She had a gallows for hanging those guilty of murder, which crime originally meant killing a Frenchman. In medieval times, the holder of the court kept any fines that were levied, and when a man was hanged all his goods were confiscated. The King had granted the Abbess the right to hold fairs and markets and this was a profitable activity in Romsey as elsewhere. Not only did the holder levy dues on stallkeepers, but he could also hold a court of "Pie Powder" ("pieds poudre" or "dusty feet") to deal with offences committed at these events, and again the holder of the court kept the fines. The Abbess also controlled weights and measures in the town. In particular her officers checked on the amount and quality of those two basic commodities, bread and beer, and those whose goods were defective were fined.

Although within Romsey the Abbess administered the law, to the outside world she was seen as responsible for her tenants. In 1286 John le Drinkwater and other Romsonians broke into the Bishop of Winchester's deer park at Merdon near Hursley. The Bishop sent a strongly worded letter of complaint to the Abbess and asked her to ensure that they did not repeat the offence. Not only was the Abbess the ruler of Romsey, but she was an important person within the Church. She was the head of the Abbey and was answerable to the Bishop of Winchester in ecclesiastical matters, and like him she was entitled to carry a crozier. The nuns came from the greatest families in the land, but as nuns they were under the discipline of their Abbess.

However, neither their holy calling, nor their powerful relations, saved them from the terrible Black Death of 1349. Most of the nuns, their servants and many townspeople died in this attack of plague which swept through Europe and decimated the population of England. The few survivors in the Abbey had to take over the reins of both spiritual and temporal rule at a time when the peasants too had died in large numbers and there were few people to work the land. The nuns nearly starved to death but were rescued by the Bishop of Winchester, William of Edyndon. He gave them some property in Romsey from which they could draw rents and in exchange he took over the Abbey's lands at Edington,

Romsey Abbey from the north-west – before the roof and other renovations carried out by the Rev E L Berthon in the second half of the nineteenth century and the addition of the north porch in the twentieth century.

his birthplace, on Salisbury Plain.

Eventually England's prosperity was regained but Romsey Abbey never recovered its former glory. The momentum had gone out of the monastic way of life and in all houses fewer candidates came forward to be nuns and those who did, had less exalted social backgrounds. After 1349 the nuns of Romsey came from leading Hampshire families, but no longer from the greatest families in England.

From then onwards there were never more than twenty-five nuns at one time in the community, compared with ninety or a hundred before 1349. The origins of the later nuns can be seen from their surnames. Some had Hampshire surnames, such as "de Romseye", "Ropley" or "Winton" (Winchester) and others had surnames of places on the edge of Romsey, such as "Pauncefot", "Okly" (now Roke), and "Persshete" (now Spursholt).

Although the Abbey suffered a great change in the middle of the fourteenth century this did not have a long term effect on Romsey. The peasants held land from the Abbey, which they tilled, and either worked on the Abbey's land or, increasingly, paid rent for their holdings. The common fields were divided up and each holder of a parcel had to sow and harvest it within certain time limits. During the winter the fences around the fields were thrown down and animals allowed to graze. The commons were also available for grazing animals and the owners paid a fee according to the ages and numbers of beasts that they turned out. Inevitably there were problems and these were sorted out in the manor court. People let ditches become blocked, thus cutting off water to some fields and flooding others. The court instructed tenants to repair their cottages and defective hedges. It controlled the area where animals might roam, forbidding "their pigs to go and wander the streets of Romsey on penalty of 6d each time", for example.

Occasionally a dispute would go beyond the manor court to the King's court. In 1261 a dispute about stocking the common pastures at Ridge to the west of Romsey reached just such proportions. William of Stratton was summonsed by Hugo de Hoymill. If one man put too many animals on a pasture it reduced the feed available for the rest and the pasture itself might be damaged. It is not recorded how many animals William had been turning out to graze but the court limited him to eight oxen, six pigs and twenty sheep. The manor court administered the rules for the passing on of tenancies. When a tenant died, his successor paid a heriot or fee to be allowed to inherit the property and swore an oath to be faithful to the

King John's House (c. 1240) and Tudor Cottage (c. 1550) are set back from Church Street up a footpath by the Post Office. They are open to the public in the summer months and visitors can explore a unique medieval building with its "Tudor modernisation".

Abbess as Lady of the Manor. Thus in 1504 Edward Alderigge, who rented lands in central Romsey, paid a heriot of one horse, worth twenty pence. At the same court it was reported that Margery, widow of Thomas Bulle, had remarried and so forfeited her late husband's holding in Spetilstrete, which is now Winchester Road. Therefore Thomas's son, John Bulle, paid the necessary fine and took over her holding of two cottages with gardens.

The tenants were by no means equal. Some had big holdings and others very small ones. Some peasants held no land of their own and worked entirely for other people. The names of some of the wealthier peasants have survived through the centuries because of written records of their transfers of parcels of land. The early documents are disappointing because, although they tell names of people, they are vague about the location of the land. In 1228 Robert and Edith de Depeden transferred two acres of land and a field in Romsey to Walter, son of Roger. In 1256 William le Paumer granted two dwellings in Romsey to Matilda del Ok. One of the dwellings lay between the holdings of Philip Athtrich and John le Blaketourer. Palmer is still a common surname in Romsey but we shall never know where this particular one lived seven centuries ago.

By Tudor times the wealthier farmers made wills and these show what sort of goods they owned. John Ray was a farmer at Cupernham who died in 1588. In his house he had a hall, two chambers and a kitchen in which there were nine flytches of bacon. Outside was a stable, a barn and standing crops. His stock included "five horse bestes and the apparell", a cart, a plough, cows, pigs, sheep, hay, vetches, grain and two stalls of bees. He left his three daughters each a cow, two bushels of wheat, and two of barley and he left lambs to various other children.

Romsey in the Middle Ages was clearly a prosperous community. However, it was not self-sufficient any more than was any other town of its time. Its main trade link was with Southampton. Woollen cloth was dyed and sent there for export, the tanners sent leather and the bakers bread. From Southampton, Romsonians bought a wide variety of goods, food, building materials and raw materials for industry.

The most plentiful food was fish. In 1443 Richard Bele brought herrings, salmon, hake, mulvel and ling to Romsey. He also brought onions, figs and dried fruit. Another merchant, John Bole, brought almonds, dried fruit, raisins and wine, which included malmsey and bastard. His merchandise was varied for he also brought a "barrel" of nails for fixing lathes on battens, while John Grenfylde of Skidmore, to the south of Romsey, brought in several thousand slates.

However the most important and largest group of goods was for industry. There were materials for wool dyeing and processing, such as madder, woad, oil, soap, weld and alum. There were teasels for raising the nap on the cloth after it had been fulled (that is, shrunk and stretched) and there were canvasses for wrapping woolfells (untreated sheepskin). William Smith, John Somerset and John Medmore between them brought in 37 hundredweight of iron and a good deal of coal, thus showing that Romsey was continuing the Saxon tradition of iron working. The tanners brought in hides and, rather surprisingly, malt was brought from Southampton. In a farming area such as Romsey, one would expect sufficient malt to be produced locally, even though ale was the normal drink of the time.

Tanning was obviously important in Romsey all through the Middle Ages and the industry only ceased in the town in the twentieth century. The master tanners were prosperous men who played a leading role in the town. One such was William Raynoldes, who died in 1579 while Mayor of Romsey. His house consisted of a hall, a parlour, a chamber, a servant's chamber, a buttery, a larder, and a kitchen. In his kitchen, at his death, were sixteen flitches of bacon, "a half hundredth" of cheese, and "certain old trashe". He had a feather bed and a bolster, with ten pairs of sheets, coverlets, and three towels. In the servants' bedroom was a flock bed and coverlets of "list" which were strips of material, originally selvages. His tanhouse contained a bark mill, a cold rake and a load of bark. In traditional tanning the skins were soaked in oak bark solution and the hair scraped off them. It was a slow, smelly and messy job. Mr Raynoldes had leather in vats, calf skins and dried leather apart from other necessaries. His professional effects were valued at £48.4s. which was a third of his total wealth.

The farmers and tanners were solid and useful men in the community but the clothiers undoubtedly brought the most money to the town. Romsey was in a very convenient position to receive wool or cloth from

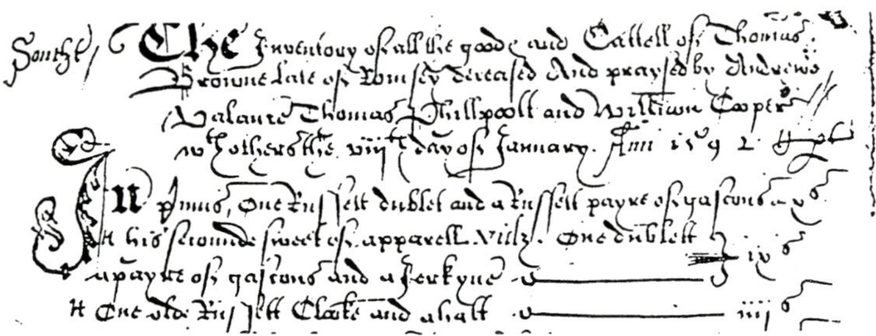

Inventory of Goods of Thomas Browne late of Romsey Deceased . . . 1592.

Town Mill, Bell Street. Later known as Dukes Mill, it was destroyed by fire in 1970. Sketch by Val Grace.

the chalk uplands, to process it and then to forward the finished product to the coastal outlet of Southampton which had a privileged link with Italian merchants. Romsey clothiers were the men who dyed and finished the woven wool. Because water was plentiful in Romsey, there was an adequate supply for these processes and to work the mill wheels of the fulling mills. In these the cloth was soaked in fullers earth and beaten with hammers to felt it. It was then racked or stretched back to the required length. In order to boost home industry the thirteenth and fourteenth century kings had made the export of raw wool very difficult and expensive. This encouraged a burgeoning weaving trade throughout England and Romsey benefited by developing the skills necessary to treat the woven cloth. Once processed, it went to Southampton where it was bought and exported by Italian merchants. In 1450 there was so much dissatisfaction with the prices paid by the Italians that the men of Romsey marched to Southampton to give vent to their feelings. However, the militia was called out and they were arrested and sent for trial in Winchester.

Notwithstanding this disagreement with the Italians, and even after the Italians ceased trading in Southampton, it was the clothiers who were the richest merchants in Romsey, ahead of both farmers and tanners. One such clothier was Richard Puckridge who died in 1614. In his shop he had four looms and in his wool loft he had £254 worth of wools, including red wool, green wool, ordinary wool, coarse wool and worsted yarn. He had four thousand tiles in the "backside" of his house and he owed thirty shillings "to the town by the collection for Middlebridge". He also owned a Bible unlike his Tudor predecessors.

Thus during these centuries the town developed a trade and industry that was independent of the Abbey. Meanwhile the Abbey itself never recovered from the Black Death. Monasticism became less fashionable throughout England and fewer candidates came forward to join the abbeys and monasteries. Rich men and women were more likely to endow chantries where masses were said for their souls, than to endow places in monasteries. In the 1330s Nicholas de Brayesfeld (or Braishfield) and Emma his wife gave lands to the Abbey and the income from those lands was used to pay a chaplain in the Abbey to say masses for the souls of the Brayesfeld family.

Although monasticism was less fashionable, it was still important in medieval life and the pious still made gifts to the Abbey. But from the fourteenth century Romsey received no more royal bequests, only the humbler gifts of lesser men. These gifts were of individual houses or a few acres of land, but in total the rents from them were a useful supplement to the Abbey's income, which had declined in value over the centuries.

Obviously the Abbey's main purpose of providing a sanctuary for women who wished to devote their lives to the service of God, continued. However, it is arguable that it became less effective. The original tenets of the Benedictine rule divided the day into prayer, work, study and sleep. Prayer continued, although there were occasional complaints by bishops of nuns missing services or gabbling them. Manual work was never a

King John's House   Discovered in 1927 converted into two cottages this upper hall house was probably built for a rich merchant in the middle of the 13th century, the principal building of a complex also containing kitchens, stables, barns and servants' hall. On the plastered walls of the upper hall graffiti scratched by members of the retinue of Edward I in 1306 can be seen, including a caricature of the king himself. The building still retains its original roof timbers and the architectural details on the exterior enable this reconstruction drawing to be produced.

feature of life for nuns although many English nuns did excellent embroidery and it is likely that those in Romsey were similarly talented. Study was more complicated. In Saxon times nuns were expected to read Latin and some of them could write it. Thus they had real scholarship to offer the children who came to them to be educated. As the Middle Ages progressed, it was increasingly thought to be unsuitable for women to read and write. They lost their literacy, they lost the knowledge of Latin and then like the other upper classes, they stopped talking in Norman French and used English. They continued to bring up children but they could no longer give them a proper education. The nuns seemed to suffer from boredom. The children were obviously a comfort to them although now individual nuns contracted privately to bring up individual children rather than maintaining a formal school. There were complaints made about male children in the nuns' dormitory and about children being brought into the nuns' part of the church, especially for night services. Other nuns kept pets, such as dogs or even a monkey, which is all a far cry from the early days of strict discipline which included a total restriction on the ownership of any private possessions. The monastery at Romsey Abbey lasted for well over six centuries and over all those years clearly fulfilled a great need. What brought about its end was the quarrel between Henry VIII and the Pope over the King's Divorce and the ensuing dissolution of the monasteries in England. Amongst the final victims of the Dissolution were the nuns who were evicted from Romsey in 1539 without pensions and, with one exception, lost to the view of history.

The exception was Jane Wadham, a niece of Queen Jane Seymour. Jane married John Foster, who had been the steward of the Abbey. Their marriage caused a scandal, for Jane had been a nun and John a priest, but the English church had broken with Rome and the marriage was allowed under the new ecclesiastical laws. John's position as steward meant that he knew the possessions of the Abbey and their worth. Before the Abbey

was closed he had been granted a handsome pension by the Abbess which the King accepted as a continuing charge on the estates. When the Abbey was closed, the King took all its lands for the Royal exchequer, but gradually John Foster leased or bought much of the Romsey lands. Initially he obtained them in partnership with other people but in time the partners vanish from documented history, leaving only Foster. Foster was not the only man in Romsey to benefit from the suppression of the Abbey but at the time he was the most prominent. It was customary for the roofs to be stripped off monastic churches to ensure that they could never be re-used. Had that happened in Romsey, it would have left the town with no parish church. For centuries Romsonians had worshipped in the north aisle and transept of the Abbey church. It was their only place of worship. The roof was therefore left on the church and the King sold the townspeople the building for £100. They knocked down the outer north aisle and the Lady Chapel at the east end of the church and were still left with one of the largest parish churches in England. Although they owned the whole church,which was dedicated to St. Mary and St. Aethelflaeda, Romsonians continued to name St. Lawrence as their parish church. The north transept of the church is dedicated to St. Lawrence to this day.

Thus the town that had grown up in the shelter of the Abbey had come of age. From being a settlement that depended on the patronage and protection of a powerful Abbey, it had become strong enough to survive the Abbey's downfall. There were enough men of wealth from independent trade who could join together and buy the Abbey church when the town needed them.

Through the Shadows of Civil War

The seventeenth century opened well for Romsey and was generally a prosperous time for the town despite the convulsion of civil war. The town showed that it could govern itself and that it had overcome the loss of the Abbey half a century before.

The St. Barbe family were settled at Broadlands by the beginning of the century and they were the Lords of the Manor of Romsey Infra. In 1607 King James I who had inherited the throne of England on Elizabeth I's death in 1603, came to stay at Broadlands. He came as the guest of Edward and Frances St. Barbe and his visit was marked in two ways. He planted a mulberry tree in the grounds of Broadlands and he granted a charter giving Borough status to Romsey Infra. The central part of the town which had been under the abbess's special jurisdiction was henceforth a borough. The Fishlake stream marked the boundary. Streets on one side of it, Middlebridge Street, Bell Street, the Market Place, the Abbey, Church Street, the Horsefair and Cherville Street, were all included in the new borough; streets on the other side of the stream such as Banning Street, The Hundred, Latimer Street, Love Lane and Spittal Street were all excluded, although they were all urban streets.

Romsey did not of course escape the national upheavals of the seventeenth century any more than it had avoided the disruption of the sixteenth century. The storm clouds of Charles I's dispute with Parliament gathered over the whole of England and Romsey was embroiled too. Charles I ruled independently for several years on the income from taxes which he could raise without Parliamentary consent. He revived the old medieval levy called "Ship Money" and the circumventing of Parliament's authority made it one of the most hated of his taxes. Eighty Romsonians were assessed and in 1635 they had to pay £30 in total. Most paid between 2s.6d. and 8s. but some were charged as much as £1. 2s.6d, or as little as 1s.

When war came, the two sons of Henry St. Barbe, then the owner of Broadlands, went to fight for Parliament. Francis St. Barbe died of wounds he received at the first battle of Newbury in 1643. This was the nearest major battle ground to Romsey, being just south of the Royalist headquarters at Oxford. Francis was buried in Romsey Abbey, but his brother John survived the war and subsequently became Governor of Southampton. The Fleming family, Lords of the Manor of Romsey Extra, were distant relations of Oliver Cromwell and also took Parliament's side. Hampshire itself did not see any famous battles. Probably the best known locally are the engagement at Cheriton and the siege of Basing House. Romsey was the scene of skirmishes and there was considerable disruption to everyday life. Romsonians must have, with justification, spent many a sleepless night as a succession of troops seized the town on behalf of one side or the other. Late in 1643, five hundred Çavaliers moved into Romsey. The Parliamentarian, Colonel Norton, was sent from Southampton to dislodge them. Colonel Norton's home was at Alresford, to the east of Winchester, but he also had a residence at nearby Wellow, so he undoubtedly knew Romsey well. He led his force over Middlebridge and into the Market Place early in the morning. A fracas ensued in which seven cavaliers were killed and forty men, two hundred horses and a cache of arms were captured. The Roundheads then plundered the town. The following winter the Cavaliers returned to Romsey. They left in January 1645, also plundering the town as they went and leaving neither "sheep nor hog" behind them.

Many of the houses in Romsey in the 16th and 17th centuries looked like this one in Middlebridge Street. (Drawing by Sybil Panton.)

Occupying troops traditionally misbehave and what distinguishes one army from another is how the outrages are dealt with. In general the Roundheads imposed more effective discipline than the Cavaliers. Two Roundhead soldiers were hung for murder on 10 May 1644. The execution took place publicly from the bracket outside the Swan Inn in the Market Place. (That building now houses the Conservative Club). The Roundheads had their own ways of releasing their feelings. On one occasion a group of them set about Romsey Abbey, attacking the organ and the seats, while a local preacher urged them on.

Charles I was eventually captured by Parliamentary forces in 1646. He was imprisoned for a time on the Isle of Wight and then moved to Hurst Castle near Lymington. On his way to London, to his death, he was brought through Romsey.

Whether Oliver Cromwell ever visited Romsey is not recorded but his son Richard certainly did. Richard married one of the Major family at Hursley, and when staying there would come to Romsey to worship with the Independents, one of whose ministers was Thomas Warren. He had been Rector of Houghton, a village to the north of Romsey. He rejected offers of the bishoprics of both Salisbury and Winchester in favour of being a Dissenting Minister in Romsey. He held this post for eighteen years until 1690, using a house belonging to a Mr. Thomas Burbank. The heirs of his Dissenting congregation still worship regularly in Romsey in the United Reformed Church.

Under the Charter of 1607 a Corporation was established with a mayor, six aldermen and twelve capital burgesses. The various duties of the Corporation were unpaid and often involved both considerable time and expense. These duties were therefore not always popular. The existing members of the Corporation selected replacements for vacancies and a refusal to serve meant a fine.

In the early seventeenth century a town hall was purchased for £42. It continued to be used until 1820 when it was replaced by a building near the west end of the Abbey. The old town hall building still stands, at the

The Old Swan Inn in the Market Place.

The St. Barbe monument in Romsey Abbey. (Photo: Stan Sales.)

junction of the Market Place and The Hundred, although its age is concealed under a modern facade, and nowadays it houses a greengrocery and offices. The meeting chamber was on the first floor and was decorated with coats of arms of important local people and with those of the king. The town's muskets were also stored in the town hall. The Mayor and past mayor were Justices of the Peace and held regular courts for dealing with petty crimes and disputes. "21st Sept. 1670 William Ireland, Innholder, to appear to answer for keeping idle persons in his house who threw out a chamber pot and a glass of beer on the Mayor and Corporation going to Church service" The ground floor rooms of the town hall were used as a lock-up. However, petty crimes were usually punished promptly, and not by a term of imprisonment. For example, in 1674 a man called Hawkins was paid 1s.8d. for whipping five vagabonds.

The Corporation also regulated trade, with a view to preventing undue or ruinous competition in the town. The number and type of shops were controlled, and there were strict rules regarding the setting up of businesses. Outsiders had to pay a substantial deposit before they might practice their trade, and these deposits were repaid if they fell on hard times. The Corporation papers record that "1684 – Gave unto

Batholomew Hunter being now reduced to poverty, the sum of £5 which he formerly paid for his freedom". In fact a byelaw of 1668 stated "No person within the town shall sell but except licensed by the Mayor".

The Mayor was Clerk of the Market and as such was responsible for its conduct although the Lord of the Manor was still entitled to market dues. The Corporation provided a bull for the town's sport of bull baiting, and had to buy the necessary rope, collar and bull ring. They also had to buy lead weights as an anchor for the rope. Once the animal was deemed to be past its prime, the butchers arranged for it to be baited to death, on the grounds that this would render the meat more tender. The Corporation encouraged the practice well into the eighteenth century, when notices were put up in the town in 1789 stating that "No bull shall be baited on 5th November as usual this year".

When the monarchy was restored in 1660 there were various demonstrations of loyalty to the king, Charles II. However, the town's accounts suggest that the biggest celebration was held for the accession of his brother James in 1685. 2s.6d was spent on changing the king's name on the Royal Coat of Arms in the Town Hall and £1.10s. was spent on "12 yards serge for a table carpet for the Town Hall". "Wine, beer, tobacco, music and other things upon the proclaiming of the king" cost the town £18.11s.2d. It must have been a big party for, by comparison, the town schoolmaster was only paid £6.13s.4d for the whole year.

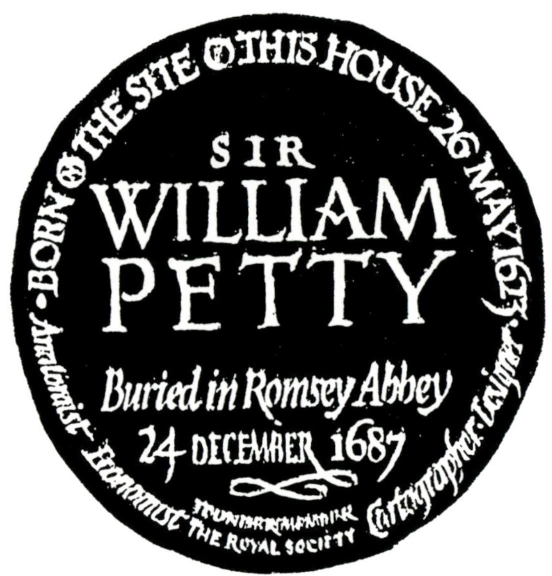

In war time, many lives are upset and people lose their livelihoods and their incomes. However, there are always a few who prosper and grow rich as a result of the upheavals around them. One such man was William Petty. His family were clothiers who lived in a substantial Tudor house in Church Street, opposite the end of Portersbridge Street. The house was burned down in 1826 but drawings of it survive. He probably received his early schooling in Romsey, before attending university both on the Continent and at Oxford. He served Cromwell in Ireland where he was a physician to the army and "surveyor of lands forfeited by rebellion". As a result of judicious investments and land purchases he became very wealthy. After the Restoration of the Monarchy he continued to be a leading figure in the scientific world and was a founder member of the Royal Society. He was knighted for his services and his descendants were ennobled, taking the title Marquis of Lansdowne.

His lengthy will sets out in detail both his philosophy and where his money was made. It is an amazing piece of self-justification. He was unusual for his time in that he did not see private charity as a way of dealing with poverty. He sets his arguments out thus, "As for beggars by trade and election, I give them nothing. As for impotents by the hand of God, the public ought to maintain them. As for those who have been bred of no calling or estate, they shall be put upon their kindred. As for those who can get no work, the magistrates shall cause them to be employed ...... I am contented that I have assisted all my poor relations ...... Nevertheless to answer custom ...... I give twenty pounds to the most wanting of the parish where I die". He believed that education was a way to help people become financially independent and his bequests included provision for four 12 year old girls and ten boys to have a year's schooling each. He died in 1685 leaving an estate worth £46,412 which, he estimated, produced an annual income of £6700! There is a nineteenth century effigy of him in Romsey Abbey.

Another Romsonian who made good, although less spectacularly than Petty, was John Kent. Unlike Petty he had a poverty-stricken childhood and often depended on the kindness of a woman neighbour for food. In due course, he made his way to London and a fortune in the silk industry in Whitechapel. Then he returned to Romsey where he became Mayor. He never forgot the kindness of the woman who had fed him as a child and set about repaying the debt he felt, by building four almshouses for widows. He died in 1692 before they were fully built. He left enough money for them to be completed and for each of the widows to receive 40s. a year. In his will he left the almshouses and the money "to be upon trust only for the poor people of the town of Romsey .... for whose benefit and better support and livelihood I intend the said premises and the yearly profits thereof for ever". His trust survives to this day and Kent's almshouses are to be found near the river end of Middlebridge Street.

The Dissolution of the Monasteries had disrupted the traditional arrangements for the care of the poor, and their numbers were swollen by discharged soldiers and those dispossessed by the Tudor enclosures of land. They alarmed the authorities who sometimes punished them and at other times made provision for them. In 1601 the various Tudor Poor Laws were codified into legislation which made each parish responsible for its own poor. In Romsey the management of the poor was a several faceted matter. Apart from private charitable efforts, the Corporation had certain responsibilities as did the Churchwardens. Both bodies had been left certain bequests for "the relief of the poor", which they had to administer. These bequests were often in the form of land, which was used as an investment to provide the necessary income.

The Corporation also put effort into preventive methods during the seventeenth century. They apprenticed pauper children, as a way of helping those children to become self-sufficient adults. Various traders, especially ale house keepers, were made to take poor child apprentices as a condition of their licence. These apprenticeships did not always work out well: "21st Sept 1670 – Ordered that Eliz. Loder, apprentice to John Hache be sent home to him again, and John Hache is ordered to receive her or else the Mayor is desired to bind him over to the next sessions". There were also strict rules to prevent poor visitors staying in the town lest they became a charge on the rates and transgressors were fined. In time these rules became a constriction on the mobility of labour because they were so widely and rigorously applied.

The main responsibility for the relief of the poor lay with the Churchwardens. They also levied rates when necessary and unlike the Corporation they had to cope with the poor of Romsey Extra as well as Romsey Infra. The Church had always been involved with the care of the poor. One of the conditions of King Edgar's Charter had been that the nuns should distribute £20 annually to thirteen needy women and seven

The house in Church Street where Sir William Petty was born. (From a drawing by Dr. J. Latham in early 19th century.)

needy men. This charity was still extant when the Abbey closed. The beneficiaries then existing were supported for the rest of their lives, but as they died the charity was extinguished.

The Churchwardens were also responsible for the upkeep of the Parish Church. They were not always conscientious in the duty, for by 1602 the building was in a very bad state and the bishop instructed them to repair it. They levied a rate to pay for the repairs and the bishop decreed that any who refused to pay would "fall under ecclesiastical law". Twenty years later the separate bell tower was dismantled and the church bells rehung in the Abbey tower. A ringing chamber was built high up above the crossing of the church and the Jacobean painting on the underside of its floor can still be seen from the nave.

The vicars of Romsey were appointed by the Bishop of Winchester and relations between the vicar and churchwardens were not always cordial. The most public disagreement came in the eighteenth century when an elderly and much hated vicar married a young wife. The Vestry Committee saw their opportunity for revenge and took it by setting the chimes of the church clock to the tune of "A Lovely Lass to a Friar Came". Subsequently parochial peace was restored and the tune of the 104th Psalm "Praise the Lord, O my soul" was adopted instead.

An Age of Elegance and Civic Pride

Nationally this was the age of elegance when the aristocracy still had many of the advantages of their roles as feudal potentates but had lost the obligations of feudal lordship. They had great incomes, beautiful clothes and built, or rebuilt, their homes to create the historic great houses which are such an attraction to tourists in the twentieth century. Their incomes were largely derived from their estates and were much increased by the more efficient use of the land brought about by the innovations of the Agricultural Revolution. They drained their lands, experimented with selective breeding of animals and grew root vegetables so that their animals could be fed and kept alive over the winter.

By the middle of the century the inventions that led to the Industrial Revolution were changing the pattern of manufacturing. The cloth trade was transformed by the flying shuttle and the spinning jenny. New improved roads were built and canals were constructed and thus it was easier to move coal to the places wishing to use steam engines for their factories. It was expensive and difficult to carry coal or heavy machines to the South of England and the industrial centre of gravity moved from the South and West to the Midlands and the North.

The century opened quietly enough. The Civil War was long gone and the monarchy re-established on new, more acceptable terms. Although there were still some echoes of the Civil War to come, none were of major significance in England. Towns like Romsey settled down to the serious business of living life and making money, for behind the glittering apex of the very wealthy was the solid phalanx of lesser mortals with lower incomes and there was still outright poverty and destitution.

Although there is an anti-intellectual streak in the English national identity, it has always been recognised that education is the keystone of financial independence in that it gives poor children a chance to rise above their environment. Different generations have interpreted this belief in different ways, whether by Charity Schools, State Schools, or scholarships in private schools. In the early eighteenth century it was not at all unusual for wealthy men to leave money for the endowment of charity schools. It so happened in Romsey that two men, neighbours, both made such bequests and died within five years of each other. One was John Nowes of Lee and the other was Sir John St. Barbe of Broadlands.

Broadlands, rebuilt and lavishly decorated and furnished by the 2nd Viscount Palmerston in the 18th century, the residence of the 3rd Viscount (the 19th century Prime Minister) and the home of the Mountbatten family in the 20th century.

John Nowes died in 1718 and dedicated specific lands on his estate for the education of forty boys, whose parents were Anglicans, twenty in Romsey and the rest in Salisbury and Yeovil. They were to be "taught and instructed in the rudiments of the Christian religion and reading and writing well in the English tongue, and learning the Catechism, reading the Bible and Common Prayer according to the usage of the Church of England and by law established". The boys were to wear caps and gowns of blue cloth and £2 a year was allocated for each boy's clothes and £1 for his tuition. In addition money was provided for apprenticeship fees.

Sir John St. Barbe died five years later in 1723. In his will he laid a charge of £25 a year on his farm of Broadlands for educating ten Romsey boys. Part of the money was to pay the schoolmaster, part was to clothe the boys and part was for the "expense of putting them out to service". Two separate schools were maintained from the incomes of these two charities and it seems probable that at least some of the beneficiaries became men of more wealth than they would have been, had they not had some education and an apprenticeship behind them.

However, not all poor boys escaped poverty in their adult lives and other people were reduced to poverty for a variety of reasons. Money to relieve the sufferers came either from charitable bequests or from the rates. In Romsey, as in other places during the seventeenth and eighteenth centuries there were several bequests of land, the income from which was to be used partly for the benefit of the poor and partly for either the mayor or the vicar. Such lands were usually left in trust to the corporation although some was left to the churchwardens. The other source of income for either churchwardens or the corporation was rates. Rates were a fixed amount, but could be levied as many times as were needed in a year. Thus in 1747 the total of the Poor Rate was £7.5s.9d., but by the time it had been levied forty times, £291.10s. was raised.

For comparison, at that time, a day's work by a carpenter cost 1s.8d. and two inch plank was 4d. a foot. A quart of strong beer was 3d., a bottle of wine for the sacraments 2s.6d. and the hire of a horse and cart for a day 2s.6d. The schoolmaster received £6.6s.8d. a year, 15,000 bricks cost £1.2s.6d. and 15,000 tiles £1.4s.

Provision had to be made not only to feed and clothe the poor but also, on occasion, to house them. By mid-eighteenth century it was thought generally that work, with a "training" element should be found and in 1747 the administrators of the poor decided to convert the "poor houses" in Newton Lane (off Bell Street) into a "workhouse". By 1766 this building was unsatisfactory and another was rented at £13 a year " to make a place for the poor of Romsey Infra", and by 1816 the building now known as King John's House was the workhouse. The management of the workhouse was normally put out to tender. In 1767 Jeremiah Major was master and undertook to find "meat, drink, washing and lodging, but not apparel, for 1s.8d. per head per week". Furthermore the churchwardens agreed to provide "an oven and a house for peat ashes". Peat was the fuel of the poor for centuries in Romsey. Dr. Latham, Romsey's late-eighteenth century historian, comments that peat "is dug in quantities at a very small distance from the town in many places".

This method of caring for the poor by tender broke down completely during the 1790's when the wars with France caused food prices to soar. In 1792 William Watts agreed to "take the poor (of Romsey Infra), and provide them in all respects for three years at £555, £540 and £535. Meanwhile Richard Withers undertook to care for the poor of Romsey Extra at £1000 per annum. However, neither Watts nor Withers would tender again in 1794 and Charles Jewell undertook Romsey Extra for £1100 a year. He gave up the contract after three months and Richard Withers agreed to resume the post for £1239.19s.6d a year, but with a ceiling on what County rates he would have to find, and a limitation on certain other expenses.

Some documents called "Settlement Certificates" survive and these tell something of the life stories of the very poor between 1790 and 1810. For example, William Fowler's story is recorded. At the time of his application he was unemployed and destitute. He had been a weekly servant to the miller, Benjamin Chandler, receiving 4s. a week plus board and lodging. After three months his pay was increased to 12s. a week but he had to "find himself in victuals, the said Benjamin Chandler providing him with small beer and lodging in the loft over the stable".

The only women mentioned in these documents are those without husbands. Not untypical of one group referred to as "single women" was Sarah Lawrence who had been a servant of Mrs. Ann Brice of Southampton at £4 per annum. She was then hired to William Sharp, a paper maker, at five guineas a year and "is now with the child that is likely to be born a bastard".

However, other classes of women such as widows or spinsters also required help when they became unemployed. One such was Mary Budden. In 1790 she had been hired to Thomas Webb, a victualler of Romsey Extra, at a wage of 1s. a week plus board and lodging. "After a year she became a domestic servant to Mr. Taylor on monthly wages. She entered into his service when he entered into the Swann Inn there and left the same when he left the said inn".

In earlier centuries many of the functions of twentieth century local councils were dealt with either by charitable provision or by some specially convened body. One such body was the Court Leet. This was a medieval court but it survived until the 1830s. By the eighteenth century it was rather feeble and had little power to enforce its decisions. The Court met annually at one or other of the town's leading inns and the proceedings included a dinner. The eighteenth century records show that it dealt with blocked ditches, heaps of dung, and unsafe chimneys; some of the same complaints were raised for several years running. Gateways blocked by carts, and roads blocked by heaps of timber were also

Bartlett's Almshouses in Middlebridge Street in early 19th century. (From a drawing by Dr. J. Latham.)

"presented" to the Court. One ropemaker went so far as to set up chains in Newton Lane in order to carry on his trade and the court ordered their removal. The fines of this court were paid to the Lord of the Manor, who had to bear certain expenses in consequence. He, through his steward, would call the court meetings. He had to provide a pound for stray animals, and a ducking stool and whipping posts for use in punishing offenders.

The upkeep of bridges was always a matter of concern and often of considerable expense. Of the two largest bridges in the locality the upkeep of Middlebridge was maintained by the County ratepayers, but that of Greatbridge to the north of the town, was an expense borne by the ratepayers of the Borough of Romsey. Repairs to Greatbridge appear at intervals in the Borough accounts. In 1688 major repairs were effected for £12.9s. In 1778 £69.5s.8d. was expended as follows:

11 loads and 1 ft of oak timber, delivered, at £3.10s a load	£38.11.4d.
1 load and 16ft of ditto at £3.2s.6d per load	4. 2.6d.
1 round stick of oak 16ft at 1/6d	1. 7.0d.
Stephen Butt, carpenter, for building the bridge	17.13.0d.
John Brookman, for ironwork	3. 1.0d.
Mr Edw. Beare for beer for the workmen	3.17.9d.
William Cole for 3 days work	4.6d.
Joseph Baker for ditto	4.6d.
Henry Butt and two men for 1 day	4.1d.
	£69. 5s.8d.

Greatbridge was extensively repaired again in 1887 when the work cost £212.14s.11d., of which timber alone cost £110.5s.9d.

Middlebridge was also rebuilt in 1783. The old three-arch bridge which had become decayed and dangerous was replaced with a single span bridge. It is likely that the pressure to repair both bridges came about because the new turnpike roads generated more traffic. Travellers were not going to use the fine new roads if they were unable to cross the rivers

Middlebridge after rebuilding in 1783.

The Cornmarket, known in earlier days as the Pig Market. The Dolphin has a Regency facade on an older structure.

in safety.

The Turnpike Trusts, who built new roads and improved old ones, all followed similar patterns. A Trust was formed of local landowners, clergy and possibly tradesmen, who petitioned Parliament to be allowed to repair their chosen roads. The existing roads would probably be described as "very narrow and ruinous and cannot by ordinary methods of repair be effectually amended, widened and kept in repair". A witness would state that he knew the roads in question and they were as described. Once Parliamentary approval was granted, the new trust would carry out a survey of its roads and would widen, straighten and repair as necessary, and in places build new stretches. The Trustees recouped their outlay by charging travellers who used the roads on a scale depending upon the length of journey and the type of traffic.

One piece of new road constructed in this way is the Straight Mile at Ampfield on the Romsey to Winchester road, now the A.31, which was built in 1758. The Winchester Trust who built this road also improved Botley Road and the way to North Baddesley. The first turnpike road in this area ran from Whiteparish to Southampton, and is now classified as the A27. It was built in 1755 and provided a good route to Salisbury instead of the old winding way. The Stockbridge Trust appears to have been the least competent local body. No milestones have been found on their roads, although they were legally obliged to provide them, and in 1850, 85 years after the Trust was formed, they did not know the length of the road in their care. Like other Turnpike Trusts, they set up toll gates for the collection of dues, but in 1857 they were 41 years in arrears of payment of interest on the initial loan capital.

A little after the new roads were built, the canal was planned. It was eventually constructed from Andover, through Romsey, to Redbridge on the outskirts of Southampton in 1794. In some parts of the country canals opened up the hinterland for the carriage of goods on a scale that stimulated major industrial development. The canal through Romsey was useful for the transportation of heavy, low value goods, but no great industrial complex developed from it. One benefit locally was that it was used to transport coal from the docks at Redbridge, which was a cheaper form of carriage than the overland journey. The Romsey wharf was sited opposite the modern Plaza roundabout, near what is now the Harrage. The outlet from the surviving stretch of the canal runs into the Tadburn river just south of there.

When Sir John St. Barbe died in 1723, Broadlands passed to his relation Humphrey Sydenham of Dulverton in Devon, with the proviso

The Canal Warf was to the left of this picture. The canal is still visible behind the Plaza Theatre.

The Gunville Gatehouse, where the tolls were collected on the Romsey to Southampton road.

that he sell Broadlands and other lands in Romsey "as soon as conveniently may be after my decease". This was apparently necessary because both Sir John St. Barbe and Humphrey Sydenham had large debts incurred by speculation in overseas trade, culminating with the bursting of the "South Sea Bubble". Broadlands was first leased to William Barcroft and then sold to the first Lord Palmerston in 1736.

In 1757 his grandson, the second Viscount, inherited the estate at the age of 17. This man became one of the great Whig peers of his generation and a member of a glittering and cultured group whose activities have created an aura of power and extravagance that still figures largely in the national consciousness. However, despite living on a larger-than-life scale in the national scene, the Palmerstons were not oblivious of their Romsey neighbours. Lady Palmerston, the second Viscount's second wife, used to take an interest in the town and its problems. In 1789 she provided an Industrial School for Girls, and like the two charity schools for boys it aimed to equip girls to become self-supporting. The school was open to all comers and taught needlework, reading, writing and scripture. After Lady Palmerston died, her son, the third Lord Palmerston who subsequently became Prime Minister, continued to finance the school in her memory.

One of the most conspicuous aristocratic extravagances of the late-eighteenth century was the refurbishing of their homes. The first Viscount Palmerston had improved the view from Broadlands by diverting the river Test into its present graceful curves through the Park. However, it was the second Viscount who initiated the major changes to the house and grounds. He employed "Capability" Brown who not only completed landscaping the Park, but was also involved in the design of the house, which was a more unusual project for him. The works were extensive and enormously expensive. At one stage the house was in such a state that Lady Palmerston could not live there for many months. Lord Palmerston died in 1802 and his son, also aged 17, succeeded to the title and the property. When he inherited it, there were still communal open fields quite near the house and the main Southampton road passed close by.

The statue of Lord Palmerston in the Market Place.

The Victorian Era: Revolution and Decline

The opening years of the nineteenth century brought a major change that enabled the new Lord Palmerston to strengthen and consolidate his estate. This was the Enclosure Award of 1808. New methods of agriculture and new techniques of drainage were proving the old communal farming to be inefficient. Increasingly in parishes up and down the land the Common Lands were enclosed and shared out between the neighbouring land-owners in proportion to their legal entitlements. Enclosures were sanctioned by Acts of Parliament and all followed a comparable pattern varied by the amount of dissent in the neighbourhood. After enclosure, land owners often exchanged acreages in order that their estates might become compact holdings. However, the Enclosures were of less advantage to the tenants of the landowners. The tenant of a given cottage had, by right of tenure, certain grazing and other entitlements on the Common Lands. After the Enclosure, his landlord was compensated for the surrender of those rights which the tenant had enjoyed. Thus many of the poorer people were often impoverished. Another group who suffered were the owners of small rights who could not afford to pay their share of the legal fees of Enclosure nor to fence their new lands and who were therefore obliged to surrender them. It has been argued that the Enclosures were one of the contributory factors of the disturbances of the 1820's which culminated in the Swing Riots, when the agricultural poor terrorised the countryside of Southern England.

The Enclosure Award was of considerable benefit to Lord Palmerston. Previously various people owned lands quite close to Broadlands House and the townspeople came past regularly to till their portions of the nearby Common fields. After the Enclosure these Common fields were no longer "Common" and were ceded to him.He closed the way across the river by Waldrons Bridge, south of the town, which had led from one group of common fields to another, and started the process of isolating Broadlands House from the town. The destruction of Waldrons Bridge was very unpopular, for the alternative route over Middlebridge made the journey between the southern banks of the Test considerably longer. However, as Lord Palmerston continued to buy the land near his house over the next fifty years, the public need for Waldrons Bridge disappeared.

Like the Agricultural Revolution, the Industrial Revolution helped England to become prosperous but at considerable cost to individual workers. The cloth trade moved away from the South of England leaving behind many unemployed artisans, skilled in obsolete trades. In Romsey the cloth trade had largely declined by 1760 and the last woollen weaver closed his doors in the 1820s. Unlike some towns in the West of England, Romsey did not diminish until only a small village remained. It found alternative work and remained a viable town. There was paper making, sack making, grain milling, brewing, and tanning, apart from the trade generated by the market. In 1825 it was stated that, "Forty men are employed in the paper works at 20s. a week on average and 60 women at 5s. At the sacking manufactury there are sixteen men who earn 15s. a week and twenty-two women 4s.6d". This was at a time when the agricultural labourers reckoned they needed 10s. or 12s. a week for bare subsistence wages.

Provision for the needy continued to be made, in part by private charitable bequests, although as the century progressed a greater part was played by communal aid through the State. The last person to provide solely for a specific charity in Romsey was John Bartlett, who had been a doctor all his life. He built six almshouses in Romsey in Middlebridge Street, almost opposite Kent's Almshouses, in 1807. When he died in

Bartlett's Almshouses moved from Middlebridge Street to Abbey Meads in 1934.

Baptist Church in Bell Street built in 1811.

1817 he left £6700 in 3% Consols to endow them, and the remainder of his estate was to be invested in public funds, the interest therefrom to be paid to the Salisbury Infirmary and the County Hospital at Winchester. The almshouses were moved to Abbey Meads in the 1930s, and the charity still exists as does that of Kent's almshouses.

In the eighteenth and nineteenth centuries, the churches and chapels played a substantial part in the provision of education. Children were taught in both day schools and Sunday schools and reading and writing were viewed not only as a way to a job, but also as the gateway to the Scriptures. At what point religious dissent became an important strand in Romsey's life is not certain, although it was clearly there by the Civil War of the 1640s. When looking at the Nonconformists, it is important to remember that the Anglicans were always the largest single congregation. The townspeople bought the abbey church; restored it at intervals, altered the interior on many occasions; and, until the 1850s, when the new cemetery for Anglicans and Nonconformists was provided in the Botley Road, most of them were buried in its churchyard. Although there are many elements in the town's religious life, the abbey has always been pre-eminent.

Nonetheless the contribution of other denominations to the town's history is important and their chapels, built in the nineteenth century are still mostly extant. One that has gone is the Independent Chapel which was built of brick in 1804. It replaced an earlier chapel on the other side of Abbey Water, the site of which was then used as a cemetery. It was itself replaced at the end of the century by the church known then as the Abbey Congregational Church. The arch adjoining stands on the site of the medieval gateway to the walled enclosure of the monastic settlement.

Like the Anglicans, the Independents had received various bequests of land, the income from which helped the relief of the poor of their communion. Seven years later in 1811, the Baptists replaced their meeting house in Middlebridge Street with a purpose-built chapel in Bell Street. The new chapel cost £1800 and was funded by a loan. Repaying this loan crippled their activities for many years, for their membership was usually only between thirty and forty people. In time the debt was discharged and their congregation remains firmly established in the town. One group that did not survive were the Quakers, whose meetings ceased in 1820. Their Meeting House in Narrow Lane was acquired by the Sandemanians but they, like the Unitarians, had gone before 1870.

It was not only the chapel goers who felt the need to rebuild. The nineteenth century saw an increasing awareness of the relationship between dirt and disease and revulsion from the public squalor of the eighteenth century, together with the collective will and the technology to improve matters, although not always without dissent and disagreement.

In 1811 the town's ex-mayor and local historian, Dr. John Latham, played a leading part in setting up a Pavement Commission, which undertook to pave, light and clean the streets of Romsey. As with the Turnpike Trusts, a private Act of Parliament was needed to give statutory powers to the Commissioners. A number of Romsonians objected so strongly to the concept that they sent a petition to the House of Lords asking them to reject the bill, but the petition failed, the bill became law and the Commissioners were able to start work.

Their first task was to assess a rateable value for each property, so they could levy a rate. They were deluged with appeals against assessment and cases of continuing dispute went to the Quarter Sessions in Winchester. Thomas Purchase's case gives the flavour of many appeals. His arguments were that "the actual rent of his house (the Bell Inn) was £15 a year. There was very little business done at his house and the Angel (a little higher up Bell Street) was rated much lower in proportion. His stables also were too highly rated at £14 a year. He had room for 18 horses only". The outcome of the appeal has been lost, unfortunately. One of the next matters to be reviewed was that of the Town Hall. The Corporation still used the Town Hall they acquired in the 17th century, which stood at the junction of the

Market Place and The Hundred. This was augmented by the rooms over the Audit House. The Audit House stood in the middle of the Market Place and comprised a first floor room with an attic above, standing on brick pillars, so that at street level, shelter was given to market traders. It had been provided in 1744 by the first Lord Palmerston in his capacity as the Lord of the Manor. By 1820 the Audit House was in "a ruinous condition" and the Corporation purchased a house to the west of the Abbey for all their needs. They relinquished their old Town Hall and the Audit House was pulled down, which left the market traders with no shelter from the weather.

One of the functions of the Pavement Commissioners, but not of the Corporation, was to light the streets. This they did by the provision of oil lamps. However, when the Romsey Gas and Coke Company was formed in 1834, some of the lamps were converted to gas. The Gas Company contracted to light the town by gas or oil for three years at £57 a year. The Gas Works was in Love Lane and the gas mains gradually extended all over the town. One of the problems was that in cold weather the gas pressure would drop and lights furthest away from the Gas Works would go out. When oil lamps were converted to gas, those with wooden lamp posts were often troublesome and unsafe and had to be replaced. The renewal each year or so of the street lighting contract was often preceded by robust negotiations. The town was never without gas lamps but there were times when they came close to it. The shops were the main consumers of gas for lighting, and such was their importance that when half-day closing was introduced in 1894 the decreased use of gas caused a sharp drop in the profits of the Gas Company.

The 1830s saw the first fruits of the long campaign for modern democratic government. In 1832 the franchise was extended to many more ratepayers and the Parliamentary constituency boundaries were revised to take account of the numbers of new voters. Three years later a Royal Commission on Municipal Corporations prepared a report on the old incorporated boroughs. Romsey was one of these and the Corporation's constitution was, like that of 177 other towns, changed to one where the councillors were elected instead of appointing their own replacements. No longer did the members have to be Anglicans and for the first time the ratepayers had a say in the selection of the administrators of the borough and the field from which those men could be selected was much extended. There were proposals to extend the boundaries of the borough to take in the whole town, but they were not adopted.

The demand for education continued throughout England and once again local demand outstripped the provision. In the 1830s two new boys' schools were built in Middlebridge Street. A Boys National School was built at the west end of the street next to Bartletts Almshouses. In National schools the religious education was Anglican, unlike the comparable British and Foreign schools where it was non-denominational. The St. Barbe charity was attached to this school, as £25 a year was no longer enough to support an independent foundation. The Nowes charity, which was based on income from land, had benefitted from the increase in rents. The Trustees amassed sufficient money to build a new school. They built a flint-clad edifice in Middlebridge Street which is now a private house. The house next to this school was occupied by a tailor who sat and worked all day in the window. He frequently rescued schoolboys from the stream which still runs beside the street, but was then much deeper and swifter as it was used to turn several mill wheels. The Town Council gave him public recognition for his life-saving efforts.

In 1846 a British school was opened in The Hundred next to the new Primitive Methodist Chapel. It was a joint effort by the Nonconformists of the town to provide non-sectarian education for their children. Florence Nightingale's father and sister both played a part in the establishment of this school. A few years later the Anglicans, led by the Vicar, the Rev. Gerard Noel, raised the money to establish an Infants National School. The Vicar died before it was built, and in his memory, his family provided extra money to build a larger structure which would also house a Girls National School. The two schools were opened in 1851 and the building is still part of the Romsey Abbey Junior and Infants School. There was a continuing interest in girls' education; even in 1839 there were 114 pupils in Lady Palmerston's Industrial School in Church Street, with three teachers. Once the new National School was opened, the Industrial School closed, but its spirit was continued as Lady Palmerston's Industrial Class. This was a special class open to those pupils who had done well lower down the school, and it had the advantage of being subsidised.

Another administrative reform of the 1830s was in the management of the poor. In 1834 the Poor Law Amendment Act ended the parish basis of poor relief and established Poor Law Unions, consisting of groups of parishes. Each Union was administered by an elected Board of Guardians answerable partly to the ratepayers and partly to central government. The 1830s were a time when the poor were in a rebellious frame of mind. The Swing Riots had been provoked by grinding poverty and starvation and took the form of smashing threshing machines, which removed a traditional winter employment from agricultural labourers. The riots were widespread in Hampshire, and Romsey did not escape. The resentments that led to these riots were still active in 1834 and the new policy of stopping outdoor relief and of providing for the poor in

The Gardens – the 19th century workhouse.

workhouses did nothing to placate the hostility of the recipients. In 1851 Joshua May's speech on being re-elected Chairman of the Board of Guardians told of earlier troubles. His speech is interesting because it not only tells of early difficulties but sets out his philosophy of making the poor self-reliant by providing them with less support. The minutes of that meeting record:- "He contrasted the early difficulties experienced in administering the New Poor Law with the quiet character of the present time. Formerly it was only under the protection of the police that Guardians could attend their duties free from violence. Since then, striving to destroy the innate principle of pauperism, the amount given was fifty per cent less, and he would ask, were the poor worse off? On the contrary, with the exception of isolated cases, the poor were happier because dependent on their own exertions".

The minute book is very revealing in that it shows the wide variety of types of hardship and how the Guardians sought to deal with them. An example of their thinking is shown in the case of Widow Read. She complained of her reduced allowance, but the Board reprimanded her and took away her relief altogether on the grounds that her son, who was earning 12s. a week, could support her. An old man of 81 had his allowance cut from 2s. 6d. a week to 2s. because the price of bread had fallen below 20d a gallon and therefore he did not need the extra money anymore. The Guardians' Minute Book also gives a good idea of the prices of basic commodities. Inevitably the Guardians would not have paid full retail prices, but their June 1851 contracts show what supplies were regarded as essential, who supplied them, and their cost. They placed the following contracts, amongst others:-

J.Pearce	for bread	7¾d for an 8lb loaf
	flour	9d. a gallon
C. Bevis	good English bacon at 70 to 80lbs per side	5¾ lb.
Mr. Genge	good old skim cheese	¾d lb.
	new Cork butter	3s.6d. lb.
Mr. Perry	good Anjou tea	3s.6d. lb.
	sugar	4½d lb.
	soda	7s.6d. cwt.
Mr. J. Withers	candles per dozen	4s.8d.
	mottle soap	4¾d.
Mr. J. Drew	good fat mutton for sick paupers	5d lb.

The workhouse was just beyond the Sun Arch and at this time had about seventy inmates. One of the Guardians who took an active interest in the affairs of the workhouse was Mr Nightingale of Embley. He came to live at Embley in the 1820s and played an active part in Romsey's affairs. Meanwhile, during the 1840s, his daughter Florence was preparing to play a part in much wider affairs.

The conduct of the Crimean War shocked the nation in the 1850s. One result of the public outcry was that Florence Nightingale finally persuaded the War Office to let her take a team of nurses to the Crimea to care for the casualties. Her work there achieved international and enduring fame and laid the basis of the twentieth century nursing service.

She used the experience she gained there to revolutionise nursing and to turn it from a class of inferior domestic service into a respected profession. She became the leading authority of her day on nursing and hospital administration and continued to be consulted on hospital design for the rest of her life.

Her path to the Crimea was smoothed by Lord Palmerston. He was a politician and a statesman of international importance, who sat in the House of Commons, for he was an Irish peer and therefore not entitled to a seat in the Lords. At the outbreak of the Crimean War he was Home Secretary. However, one effect of the national outrage was the toppling of the Prime Minister, Lord Aberdeen, and his replacement by Lord Palmerston, in 1855. Lord Palmerston continued to be Prime Minister almost continuously until he died in 1865 at the age of 81. As with all who hold high political office, he had opponents, but he never made enemies of them. His strong foreign policy brought Britain not only prestige, but with it peace and prosperous trade abroad. His support of reforms to improve the lot of the poor helped make him the most popular figure of his time. Romsey people proudly welcomed him with peals of bells and triumphal arches when he became Prime Minister in 1855. He was a good landlord, making sure his tenants were well housed. He enjoyed seeing the improvement of the estate and the planting of trees, as much as the seasonal shoots.

The nineteenth century was one of great expansion of the population of England, but Romsey did not follow the national trends. For the first half of the century the town's population expanded by a third from 4274 to 5654, and thereafter was static until 1901. The population of England expanded three and a half fold in the same time, and had Romsey grown proportionately the 1901 population would have been around 14000.

There was considerable emigration from Romsey both to other towns in England and abroad, as the town's sons and daughters went away in search of work. The industries which replaced the wool trade were not buoyant enough to support an increasing population and agriculture reeled from blow upon blow after a prosperous start. The lack of work and the drain of population meant empty property and hence less income from rates, which made the administration of the town more difficult. In the end, Romsey did find economic salvation, but there were thirty or forty lean years to live through first.

The railways are generally seen as bringing prosperity but in Romsey the lean years followed their arrival. It was as if they provided a way for people to leave rather than as a carrier of wealth to the town. The railway did immediate and demonstrable damage to Romsey's trade because people who travelled by train no longer needed to stop at the town's coaching inns for refreshment. The Bell Inn in Bell Street and the Queen's Head in The Hundred closed in the 1850s and the owner of the Dolphin in the Corn Market became bankrupt. The railways themselves were major employers of labour and throughout the years many Romsonians have worked on the railway. After the Eastleigh railway works opened at the turn of the century many men from the town went to work there.

The first line through Romsey was opened to passengers in 1847. It was built by the London and South Western Railway and was a branch line from Bishopstoke (now Eastleigh) to Salisbury. The line circled the town to the east and north and much of it is on an embankment. Originally part of it was on an open wooden bridge, but after several fires the embankment was constructed. The bridge over the canal, which still survives, was built large enough to allow a horse drawing a barge to pass underneath. The Sun Arch, at the bottom of Winchester Hill was built to carry this railway line. The bridge is low and askew to the road, which is prone to flooding and was the place of several fatal accidents before high vehicles were banned from going underneath it in the 1970s. During the 1850s plans were made for the construction of a railway line from Andover to Redbridge, using the course of the canal, which by this time had almost ceased operations. The line was opened for public use in 1865.

Romsey Station LSWR, thought to be photographed in 1884.

Photo: National Railway Museum, York.

A collapsible boat built by the Rev E L Berthon's company at the end of the 19th century, being demonstrated on the river Test.

The later years of the nineteenth century saw the incumbency of Romsey's most colourful vicar, the Reverend E. Lyon Berthon, who held the post from 1860 to 1892. Besides being vicar, Mr Berthon was a talented engineer. He carried out much skilful and careful renovation of the Abbey church and generally resisted the temptation to modernise it, as was the Victorian vogue. One piece of modernisation in which he did indulge was the installation of black finned Gurney stoves in an attempt to warm the building in winter. The church has always been cool and in winter can be extremely cold. As late as the 1970s worshippers equipped themselves with blankets in severe weather. The Gurney stoves consumed vast amounts of coke but they did help to alleviate the chill.

Berthon designed a folding lifeboat and set up a factory for constructing these craft. He became one of the larger employers in Romsey. In due course he moved his works to the corner of Portersbridge Street and Latimer Street, but the boats were always tested in the river at Mill Lane. He was an energetic man, designing, among many other things, a collapsible bandstand, and organising civic functions to celebrate important occasions. Despite his civic and business interests he seems to have carried out his pastoral duties conscientiously for complaints of their neglect do not survive, if they ever existed, and after his death his life was commemorated by a stained glass window in the north transept of the Abbey.

Berthon was a great admirer of Lord Palmerston and held him in sincere regard. Palmerston helped to pay for the Gurney stoves as well as helping other local causes, especially when approached by Berthon. Berthon was truly sorry when Palmerston died in 1865 and helped to arrange local memorials. A statue was erected in the Market Place and a memorial window was put into the west end of Romsey Abbey. This was unveiled with the aid of seven pounds of magnesium flare inside the building, so that the decorative glass could be seen clearly from the outside. The window later became unsafe and was replaced by plain glass.

A more lasting memorial to Lord Palmerston survives in Mile Wall. The second railway line through Romsey ran from Southampton to Andover. In a complicated deal, Lord Palmerston made land available to the railway company and arranged for the main road to Southampton to be rebuilt half a mile east of its traditional route and hence further from Broadlands House. A wall was then built along the east and north of the Park, thus effectively isolating the House from the town. It was dubbed "Mile Wall" from its considerable length.

The Abbey and in the foreground the old Vicarage and the school, originally the Girls National School.

On Lord Palmerston's death Broadlands passed to his stepson William Cowper Temple. He was responsible for getting the "educational conscience" clause through Parliament. In 1870 education was first made compulsory, but no child was to be compelled to receive religious education against the wishes of its parents. That clause has remained on the Statute Book ever since. The effect of compulsory education was that once again educational provision in Romsey was insufficient. This time it was the boys' schools that were too small. A new National School was built in Station Road in 1872 and William Cowper Temple contributed generously towards the costs. The Nowes School was closed and the charity attached to the new school.

Although schooling was made compulsory in 1870 it was not free. The local schools were visited frequently by public-spirited wealthier members of the community and some demonstrated their goodwill by paying the fees of impoverished pupils. The school teachers – master or mistress – had not only to teach the pupils in their care, but to select, supervise and teach the monitors and pupil teachers. The pupil teachers had extra lessons either before or after school in order to prepare for special examinations. Apart from collecting the school money, sending after absentees and running a clothing club, the teachers from the National schools normally taught in the Sunday School, and even in 1896 the school mistress was only receiving £100 a year. At intervals numbers would be decimated by events in the town or by epidemic. There was a steady trickle of children, who changed from the National School to the British School or vice versa. Some notes taken from the school log book of the Girls National School illustrate the problems. The log book was written by the head mistress and the other National Schools and the British School kept comparable records.

3 Nov. 1862	School visited by Mr. Nightingale, Children particularly troublesome.
1 July 1863	Sent round quarterly accounts to those ladies who pay for children.
10 Oct 1865	Children absent gathering acorns for sale.
20 Oct 1866	Fires began.
7 Nov 1866	Fires discontinued because of suffocating smoke, room cold. Children restless.
25 Nov 1867	Two girls away because they have no shoes. Sent two pairs of old ones home to their mothers.
13 Apr. 1869	I find many are absent because their fathers are out of work and therefore cannot pay their schooling.
5 May 1871	On Monday, being May Day, and in compliance with an old custom the school went for a walk. It was pleasant to

	find that several of the older girls arrived early at school and decorated the room with cowslips and other wild flowers. (Author's note: cowslips still grow wild in a few places in Romsey.)
2 Feb 1874	Ellen Rayne left the school on account of not being allowed to pay into the clothing club as she does not attend Sunday School.
9 Nov. 1874	Only 29 children present in the morning, it being Fair Day. Gave a half holiday in the afternoon.
26 Feb. 1875	Alice Savage re-admitted having attended the British School for twelve months.
29 Sept. 1876	Attendance not good as several children are away with mumps and the monitor with erysipelas.
12 Dec. 1879	Martha Pitt taught for the last time as pupil-teacher. She intends entering Salisbury College after Christmas.
24 Dec. 1879	Children and teachers presented Martha Pitt with a very nice work box. (Three years' later Martha Pitt gained a First Class Certificate as a teacher.)
3 Dec 1883	School closed because of measles epidemic.
19 Oct. 1885	Ethel Millar died of whooping cough.

It is very noticeable from a study of these school log books that, gradually, the health of children has improved in the last hundred and fifty years.

The upsurge in the demand for education saw the provision of a number of private schools. Some were very small and probably none too competent, but others were more substantial. Two stand out. The first was the school in the Harrage. In its heyday it was owned and run by Mrs. Godwin Withers, and for a time used the grandiose title of the "South of England Educational Home for Young Ladies". It existed for nearly half a century until the 1890s, but has left very little trace in the town's folk memory, as it mostly catered for boarders from outside the town.

John Frederick Osborne's school for boys, Osborne House, made far more impact. In the 1860s he built a school in Church Street, since demolished and replaced by a car park, and moved his school there from Lansdowne House in Church Path. This school lasted until the 1930s and many of the sons of the town's business men were educated there, as well as boarders whose homes were in outlying villages, in Southampton, or even abroad.

Two other substantial edifices were also built in the 1860s when it was decided to erect a purpose-built Town Hall and Corn Exchange. However, the needs of the two buildings could not be reconciled, so a Town Hall was built on the south side of the Market Place and a separate Corn Exchange in the middle of the road facing The Hundred. Lord

Palmerston helped to finance the new Town Hall, although he died before it was completed. There was also a government grant because the building incorporated the County Court. When the new Town Hall was opened in 1866 the building to the west of the Abbey was no longer used by the Borough Council, but it continued to be put to community use until it was replaced by the Church Rooms in the 1960s.

The problems of diversification of powers of local government between several bodies were considerable. Romsey in the 1860s and early in the 1870s was administered, as it had been since the 1830s, partly by its elected Borough Council, partly by the self-appointed Pavement Commissioners and, for certain matters, mostly health, by the elected Board of Guardians. Each body was financed by rates which they each fixed and collected and each had different boundaries.

It meant that when a sanitation crisis occurred, there were undue problems in dealing with it and the main burden fell on the Pavement Commissioners who fortunately had some capable and interested men active in their affairs at the time. The main drainage system through the town centre derives from the Fishlake which has two branches in the town. One flows through the Horsefair brewery, down behind King John's House, between the Dolphin Yard and the Bus Station and on into Middlebridge Street. In the latter half of the nineteenth century, apart from any brewery use, it would have turned the mill wheel of the Town Mill, (now replaced by the Dukes Mill shopping precinct), provided water for the tanneries in Middlebridge Street, and power for two more water wheels. The other branch of the stream flows in front of the brewery in Church Street, crosses under the road and flows through the cellars of the houses on the west side of Church Street and the Market Place. It can be seen in Abbey Water where it used to turn the mill wheel of Abbey Mill No. 1. It then flows westward and joins a braid of the Test near the Memorial Park. A small culvert used to take water down behind the houses in Bell Street. This stream was used both as a water supply and as a drain.

In April 1876, the bank of the Fishlake stream gave way to the north of the town. Flooding was not a problem, but lack of water through the town was. The unplanned loss of water in the two channels produced a serious health hazard throughout the whole town centre, because many pumps relied on the water in addition to the people who had neither pump nor well. It took between four and five weeks to restore the water, and cost the ratepayers £12.9s.5d in unbudgeted extra expense.

At about this time negotiations were proceeding for the creation of an Urban Sanitary Authority. In 1870 Parliament decreed that every town must have such an authority, but neither the Guardians, the Pavement Commissioners nor the Borough Council felt competent to don the mantle. The issue took several years to resolve and in the interim none of these bodies would act, lest they create a precedent. The matter was resolved later in 1876 by the abolition of the Pavement Commission, the extension of Romsey Borough to cover the whole of urban Romsey, and the bestowal of the sanitary duties on the new Borough Council.

The enlarged Borough Council gradually installed storm-water drains around the town, but in 1887 the work was still far from complete. Councillor William Roles, a master plumber, made various acid comments in his diary about the inept way in which the work was proceeding. On 27th June he wrote, "The business of the meeting was so bad that I proposed the adjournment to Tuesday at 7.30 p.m. when the reports, as to drainage, should be reconsidered and in the meantime the Borough Surveyor write on clean paper a proper report with the alterations now suggested". Roles did not attend the adjourned meeting that he had proposed, but he continued to make detailed criticisms of the plans and their execution until the work was complete.

The 1880s saw a revival in Romsey's vitality after the doldrums of a generation. A tangible memorial is the fact that two chapels were built. The Wesleyan Methodists built a new chapel in The Hundred in 1883, as they found Banning Street too rough for the gentler members of their congregation. The Salvation Army took over their old chapel. The Independents, now called Congregationalists decided to replace their brick church with a stone one built with all the panache of Victorian Gothic design. Despite its grandiose exterior, the main room has an intimate and pleasing feel to it.

In the latter half of the century, three little Chapels-of-Ease were built; one at Lee, which is now an art gallery, one at Ridge (off Pauncefoot Hill), which had a school attached and is now a private house; and St. Swithun's at Crampmoor, which is still a chapel, although the attached school has gone.

The town benefited in the 1880s from the arrival quite independently of two wealthy and energetic men. One of these was William Williams. He

Gas bracket outside the Town Hall.

Timsbury Pumping Station, South Hants Water Company, which supplied Romsey with water. Photograph taken in 1911.

bought the mill in River Meads and set up in the manufacture of leather boards. After the establishment of a democratically elected County Council in 1888, he was the town's first County Councillor. By coincidence his granddaughter, Mrs. P.A. Wellington was the town's first lady Mayor in 1962. The other bringer of work to Romsey was David Faber. He was a member of the banking and publishing family of Faber and he bought the town's three largest breweries, all of which were in a poor state of management. He reorganised them under the name of the biggest of them, Strongs, and built up a successful business covering a wide area. As the result of his adoption of the business name of "Strong", the south of England was decorated in the twentieth century with the advertising slogan "You are in the Strong Country" and the Horsefair brewery bore the legend "The Heart of the Strong Country".

The capital and expertise injected by Faber, Berthon and Williams did a great deal to keep the town alive. It is noticeable that a significant number of new houses were built only after 1886. The 1860s and 1870s had seen virtually no houses built. A lasting contribution of David Faber was the renting and subsequent purchase of the Swan Inn in the Market Place after it ceased to be an inn in 1894. He made the premises available

Strongs Brewery Wagon Fleet.

as a Conservative Working Men's Club which role it occupies to this day. Romsey was well able to celebrate important national events and Queen Victoria's Golden Jubilee in 1887 was no exception. The Rev. Berthon produced the initial plans for a celebratory dinner and William Roles commented in his diary that "they were imperfect and would doubtless be found to be underbudgeted". The dinner seems to have consisted of beef, potatoes, bread and boiled pudding washed down with beer. For 2,500 people, 320 lbs of beef were cooked by the town's bakers, potatoes were boiled in baskets, partly at the Town Hall, partly at the Soup Kitchen, and partly at Broadlands. 900 l bs. of pudding were boiled in the homes of the town's leading citizens, and the whole lot taken to Broadlands for the celebration. On the day, the proceedings started with a church service, and since the diners had to supply their own cutlery, presumably each member of the congregation was equipped with his knife, fork and spoon.

Ten years later, the Diamond Jubilee was marked by the raising of funds for a local hospital, which was built in Greatbridge Road. The old queen died four years later and the news reached Romsey during a concert given in the Town Hall by local children. The news was announced, and although the concert continued, the audience gradually crept away.

Thus the nineteenth century, probably the greatest in England's history, had run its course and Romsey, like everywhere else had to turn its attention to the demands of a new era.

Twentieth Century Revival

While England as a whole had surged ahead benefiting from its advanced industrialisation, Romsey had been relatively static. It was not until the twentieth century that the town started to make up lost ground. At the beginning of the twentieth century most Romsonians earned their living within the Romsey area and the economy of the town was heavily dependent on agriculture and related trades. Romsey is still a small town, but a smarter and more prosperous one, many of whose inhabitants earn their living elsewhere. The story of Romsey in the twentieth century is the story of how the town changed from a quiet backwater to a thriving community.

These were years of extensive housebuilding in many parts of England, and in Romsey houses were built in many new places including Greatbridge Road, Mill Lane, Station Road and Winchester Road, where before there were fields. The Primitive Methodists built a new chapel in Middlebridge Street in 1893, which they occupied until their merger with the Wesleyan Methodists in the 1920s. Their Middlebridge Street chapel has remained a place of worship and is now used by the Elim Pentecostal Church. Meanwhile their old chapel in The Hundred was taken over by the Test Valley Iron Works, who used it to display farm machinery. Additional buildings were used for heavy iron and brass foundry work. At its peak this firm employed forty people; the cast iron crosses they made can still be seen in the cemetery and drain covers with their imprint are still in use in the town.

The Roman Catholics also returned formally to Romsey after a gap of several centuries. Throughout the years of religious dissent and persecution, there were few Roman Catholics in the town. In the 1890s a convent and church were opened near the Abbey. Initially the nuns provided an orphanage but since the 1930s they have run a girls' school. In 1910 the Catholics opened a large boarding school for boys in Botley Road, called Montfort College. It catered for boys who intended to enter the priesthood and continued to be used for that purpose until it closed in the 1970s.

Meanwhile the Nonconformists found it increasingly difficult to maintain their British and Foreign School in Winchester Road. Although the building had been enlarged twice it needed replacement and the County Council took over the school in 1911 with the intention, not fulfilled for many years, of building a new one. The Nowes Charity which had been attached to the Boys National school had made no payments for many years. The agricultural depression in the last decades of the nineteenth century meant there was insufficient income from the land owned by the charity. Early in the 1900s the land was sold, the money reinvested and the charity was able to make payments again.

One of Romsey's most famous inhabitants, Florence Nightingale, died in 1911. Her body was brought by train to Romsey station and the funeral procession then went to East Wellow church for burial in the family vault. Romsey's shops and schools shut for the day and many old Romsonians remember seeing the procession pass, and others have described following it on foot to East Wellow.

A prominent Victorian establishment which disappeared in these pre-war years was the Berthon Boatyard. Collapsible lifeboats had been provided on the Titanic and their failure was an aggravating feature of the disaster. After the ship sank in 1912 collapsible lifeboats were outlawed, and although Berthon boats were not the ones which failed to open in that catastrophe, they were damned with the rest. The Rev. Berthon did not see this end to his business as he had died in 1899. The Romsey boatworks closed, and was purchased by a Lymington company who continue to trade under the Berthon name, although all connection with the Berthon family has gone.

One sign of the town's continuing community spirit was the mounting of a Millenary Pageant in 1907. At the time it was thought that Romsey Abbey had been founded in 907, so a pageant of a thousand years of history seemed a fitting way to mark the occasion. The main events of the town's life were committed to verse for enactment by many of the townspeople. During the three days of performance various unemployed men were dressed as Anglo-Saxons and given the task of guiding visitors from the railway station to Broadlands, where the Pageant took place. Thousands of people came, including the Archbishop of Canterbury and many other distinguished people. Sufficient profit was made to pay for the building of a north porch on the Abbey Church.

In the years leading to the First World War, Romsey had its Volunteers and Rifle Shooting Clubs, and when war was declared, members of these organisations were amongst the first to volunteer. During the war, Romsey played host to a series of men on their way to the front, including the New Zealand Expeditionary Force, whose members wore wide-brimmed hats that are very conspicuous in the old photographs of the time. Apart from regular soldiers, a large number of Kitchener's Army of volunteers were quartered in Romsey and billeted in private houses. They had been recruited so quickly that some of them were without uniforms and wore their own clothes, which were dirty and flea ridden. Since they had nothing else to wear, these clothes could neither be cleaned nor fumigated, but baths were made available at the Workhouse.

Two Y.M.C.A. recreation huts were provided at Pauncefoot and at Woodley, which were staffed by local voluntary workers, who arranged concerts and other entertainments for the troops.

During this war, the military were still heavily dependent on horses. Hundreds of horses and mules passed through Romsey on their way to the Front via the Remount Depot on Pauncefoot Hill. It was established in 1915 and half-broken mules and horses were brought there. The trains carrying these animals would stop at two specially built sidings at Romsey Station Goodsyard. They had to be brought through the town to Pauncefoot Hill and this caused inconvenience and danger to pedestrians. They were a hazard in Romsey, but in the lanes around Ridge they caused so many obstructions that frequently pupils could not get to Ridge school. Many of the children transferred to Copythorne school and the numbers at Ridge dwindled to thirty pupils. The school never recovered and was finally closed in 1934.

Like all towns, Romsey had flag days and collections at intervals throughout the war to raise money for guns, horses or medical services. Young men joined up in great numbers, the most remarkable being eighty four men from Banning Street. This short stretch of road which ran from Middlebridge Street to the Tadburn, was in those days made up of small working-class houses with the addition of two or three courtyards of

Romsey Abbey, showing North Porch built from money donated from the proceeds of the 1907 Pageant.

Extract from "The Millenary Celebration – Words and Music". "Perhaps the most striking thing about our celebration will be found in the unanimous response which has come from every class and station in Romsey. Rich and poor, gentle and simple, Church and Nonconformist, have all worked heartily to ensure its complete success".

houses set back from the street line. The houses have all gone now and the street is partly replaced by Broadwater Road.

In fact so many men joined the Forces that by 1915, there was a serious shortage of agricultural workers. Hampshire County Council Education Committee allowed boys to leave school at twelve years, instead of the existing minimum age of thirteen, if they were going to work on a farm.

One of the appalling results of the First World War was the slaughter of a high proportion of the young men of the nation, and the resulting imbalance between men and women of their age group distorted the population figures for a long time. It is therefore interesting to see how the community closed the wounds and resumed peacetime life. A Memorial Park was opened by the river in an imaginative tribute to those who had given their lives in the war, and that park still plays its role in the town's social life.

In January 1922, the *Romsey Advertiser* made a resumé of Romsey's activities in 1921. The war was still casting a shadow, but a shadow that was beginning to soften. Captain Henry Ashley, brother of Colonel Wilfred Ashley, M.P., of Broadlands, had died of war wounds. War Memorials had been unveiled in Romsey, Braishfield and Awbridge, and local branches of the new League of Nations had been formed.

Townspeople were busy working for good causes and to help those less fortunate than themselves. The annual meetings of both the R.S.P.C.A. and the Romsey Nursing Home were reported and there was a variety of fetes and flower shows in aid of the Hospital Fund, various Friendly Societies and other deserving causes.

The Romsey Advertiser reported:

"On nearing Christmas, the Mayor, Col. Footner, D.S.O., opened a fund for the unemployed. The police organised a football match and the Romsey Rovers and Scouts gave the proceeds of an entertainment towards making poor homes of Romsey brighter."

The first public lecture in connection with the Romsey Branch of the

Abbey Mill, Abbey Water, destroyed by fire 1925. (Drawing by Val Grace.)

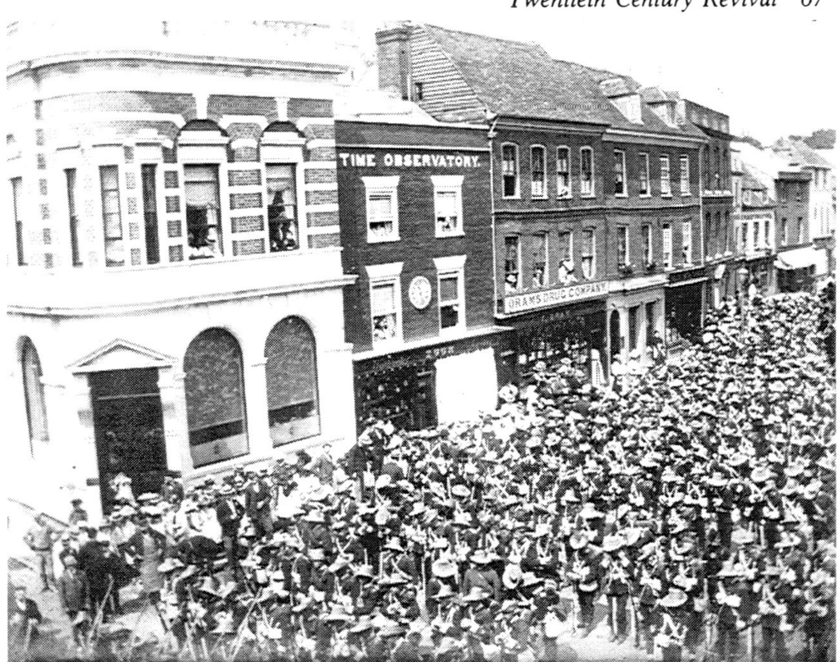

Dominion troops in the Market Place during the Great War.

Workers Educational Association was reported. Sport was again in the news: Romsey Football Club was formed: the Football Final of the Ashley Cup between Romsey Comrades and Andover Comrades was played; and the S.W. Centre of the Junior Car Club held a Rally. The Romsey Lawn Tennis Club held its summer tournament and the Southampton Rambling Club were entertained by Mrs. Suckling, Romsey's local historian, at Highwood:- "She treated them to a discourse on 'A Forgotten Past'". There was a fair at Michelmersh and the Romsey Agricultural and Horse Show Society held both an autumn and a Christmas Show.

Although the world was picking up the threads of peace, it was not picking up the threads of life as lived before 1914. Mechanisation was bringing change. Travel and communication were about to be revolutionised by buses and radio. However, motive power was in an experimental stage before the internal combustion engine became the universal mode of transport. Traction engines were still seen as a viable alternative in 1921, as the following court case illustrates. A man was brought before the Romsey Bench charged with "driving a locomotive on

December 14th in Alma Road that did not consume its own smoke and with having no communication cord on the rear wagon". (There were three wagons attached to the locomotive).

In 1926, the question of a proper sewerage system for the town was raised. The town was poor and the scheme would add greatly to the rates, but would be more hygenic than buckets that were emptied twice weekly. The local council elections were fought on the issue and the town voted to keep its buckets. However central government stepped in and within a few years, Romsey was made to instal sewers. The young mostly remembered the diver who put the pipes across the river in Mill Lane. His air supply was maintained by a hand pump and he wore a very heavy diving suit. For the adults the digging up of the town's narrow streets for months was of greater concern. The main road to Bournemouth was at that time through The Hundred, Bell Street and Middlebridge Street, so having half the road width unusable caused severe congestion. Whether it was coincidence or whether this disruption proved to be the catalyst is a matter of conjecture, but soon afterwards a bypass was built on the south between the town and Broadlands Park. Middlebridge was rebuilt in 1934 and although it still looked much like its predecessor, it was both wider and stronger and had less of a humpback.

Also during the 1930s the Plaza, Romsey's first purpose-built cinema

Romsey Tomatoes – grown in the nurseries between Botley Road and the railway line, until 1982. (Photo: Pat Sillence.)

opened, at the junction of Southampton and Winchester roads. Previously films had been shown commercially in the Corn Exchange or at the Elite Cinema, the old wool warehouse in Middlebridge Street. At this time too, the hospital in Greatbridge Road was replaced by a more modern and convenient building on Winchester Hill, and considerable effort went into the fund-raising for the venture. The older building was converted to private dwellings.

In many parts of the country the economic depression created havoc with local communities. Whereas Romsey did not escape the effect of mass unemployment, it was not ravaged by it as some places were. Strongs Brewery managed to continue to employ its staff and this meant jobs for many Romsonians. Wills Nursery in Botley Road also needed a large work force and this saved many more families from the poverty of the dole queue. The Nursery, which closed in the early 1980s, was noted for "Romsey tomatoes". The firm had the only private railway siding in Romsey and coal was brought by rail to heat the greenhouses. However, their perishable produce was taken directly to the railway station to ensure that it was sent away quickly.

Meanwhile Broadlands was still a private house. It had passed in 1865, on Lord Palmerston's death to his stepson, William Cowper, later Lord Cowper Temple. From him it passed to his relations, the wealthy Ashley family. In 1922, the young Louis Mountbatten married the heiress to the Ashley fortune, Edwina, and in 1939, on the death of her father, Lady Edwina Mountbatten inherited Broadlands, the house in which she had been born. Shortly afterwards the Second World War broke out and Lord Louis' naval position took him away to sea, and ultimately to glory as the Supreme Allied Commander of the South East Asia Command. He saw the surrender of Japanese forces and had the task of maintaining the government of countries liberated from Japanese rule. Lady Mountbatten, with bravery, enthusiasm and determination played her part by organising the release of ninety thousand Japanese-held prisoners of war and internees, in a space of six weeks.

Meanwhile in England, Broadlands was in use throughout the war. The treasures were packed up and boards put up to protect the room decorations. The house was used as an annexe to the Royal South Hants hospital, which had not escaped enemy attack. While she was in England, Lady Mountbatten, who was a leading member of the St. John's Ambulance Brigade, took a personal interest in the patients who were nursed in her home. Romsey escaped the German bombs almost unscathed, while nearby Southampton was pounded to a heap of rubble in the merciless days of 1940 and 1941. Many children were officially evacuated to Romsey and the villages around, and many adults unofficially fled the nightly bombardment. Many of them slept at North

Baddesley but others came as far as Romsey, even though some of them had to sleep in the park.

In 1944 the fortunes of war changed and Britain was able to go on the offensive. As D-Day approached, Lee House on the Broadlands Estate was used as a planning centre; the waters around the port of Southampton were full of craft including landingcraft, floating breakwaters and pontoons, and the hinterland, which included Romsey, swarmed with men and armaments.

The war brought a quite different group of soldiers to Romsey. These were Italian prisoners-of-war, whose camp was at Ganger Farm on the Braishfield Road. They were employed locally and three were detailed to work at the Test Valley Iron Works. However, they are mostly remembered for the drainage work they carried out around Budds Lane and Greatbridge Road. Although that area continued to be flooded at frequent intervals into the 1980s, their work reduced the extent of the floods very considerably.

After the war, in 1945, there was a mood for change in the country. This saw expression in the election of a Labour Government at Westminster which was committed to reform. The nationalisation of gas and electricity undertakings had a demonstrable effect in Romsey. The Gas Works in Love Lane was taken into public ownership. The plant was considered to be in a rather run-down state and the Southern Gas Board ran a new main from Southampton to supply the town, and closed the local gas works. The new Electricity Board provided a far better power supply than had previously been available and by 1979 all the town's street lamps were electric. The last shop to have gas lamps was Woolworths and although they were used as emergency lighting, they were removed in 1981.

The post-war years saw the building of many council houses. These were partly to provide additional rented accommodation and partly to replace substandard houses. The houses in Banning Street, Newton Lane and Love Lane were mostly demolished. Council houses were built in Mountbatten Avenue, Chambers Avenue and Viney Avenue, and flats were built beside the new road at the rear of The Hundred called Broadwater Road, to list just a few places. Two factors stopped this pattern of demolition and building. The conservationists pointed out that many houses need not be condemned as slums but could be renovated. They proved their point most spectacularly in Cherville Street where they have restored a row of houses that had been widely regarded as beyond redemption. The other factor that slowed down the building of council houses was that the policy of widespread provision of such homes was called into question and the political will to build them was weakened.

The 1944 Butler Education Act required that the school leaving age be raised to 15 and that all children attend secondary schools after the age of

11. Before the reorganisation, the "scholarship" children attended grammar schools at Eastleigh, Winchester or Andover and the rest were accommodated in their existing elementary schools. A secondary school was then opened in temporary classrooms, behind the Plaza, next to the railway line.

Since 1957 two new secondary schools have been built, the Romsey School and Mountbatten School; new primary schools have been built near the Plaza and at Cupernham and at Halterworth, and the Girls and Infants National Schools reorganised as the Abbey Junior School. The old British School in The Hundred was left empty for some years and is currently a private language school, and the old National School in Station Road is now the town library.

Two men stand out in borough affairs from the 1940s and 1950s. One was Alderman R.C. Chambers. He had come to Romsey in 1924 when he was appointed General Manager of Strongs Brewery. He was Mayor of Romsey throughout the war and played a leading role on the Council for many years. In 1947 he was made a Freeman of the Borough, a year after the same honour had been bestowed on Lord Mountbatten. Alderman Chambers became Joint Managing Director of Strongs in 1954 and died in 1956.

In 1968 Romsey honoured one of its longest serving councillors, Mr. Reg. Symes, by making him a Freeman of the Borough. He had been a member of the Council since 1931, an alderman since 1932, mayor several times and a J.P. The unexpected fact was that he was a leading Labour Party member and Romsey has been solidly Conservative throughout this century. He was one of those sensible people whom everyone trusts and was honoured because of the high regard in which he was held. His family have been in Romsey from at least the fifteenth century.

The railways were also nationalised by the Labour Government of 1945 but the trend towards car commuting and the lack of social or commercial links between Romsey and Andover meant that the line was closed in 1964. A few people were seriously inconvenienced despite the substitution of a bus service, and even that has since been discontinued. Romsey's other rail routes still exist although the line to Eastleigh is normally only used for freight.

By the 1950s the need for more jobs to be provided locally was apparent and an industrial estate was opened in Budds Lane. One of the companies attracted to the town was Hampshire Industrial Textiles Ltd, which is a branch of the Wilton Royal Carpet Company, and by 1980, it was the second largest employer in Romsey. The computer company IBM and the electronics company, Plessey, have both set up laboratories not far from Romsey and they have both provided work for Romsonians and brought an influx of newcomers to the area. The establishment of a single headquarters for the Ordnance Survey on the western edge of Southampton in the late 1960s had much the same effect.

Despite the new industries there has been a loss of job opportunities in the less skilled areas. Strongs were totally absorbed by Whitbread and the brewing side of the business ceased in the 1980s. Wills Nursery closed and the tomato and chrysanthemum growers lost their jobs and there have been other closures too. This represents a shift of emphasis rather than a major shrinking of opportunities.

This change of emphasis in the work available was reflected in the pattern of housing. With the mid-twentieth century trend to live in one area and work in another, many people who worked in Southampton or Winchester, came to live in Romsey, and many Romsonians continued to live in the town, even though working outside it. Old established roads, like Cupernham Lane, were lined with houses and then whole new estates were built with various types of private houses from the modest to the luxurious. The developments filled the fields of Cupernham, of Woodley and of Halterworth. Following the war Broadlands had again become a private home. Lord Mountbatten had been appointed Viceroy of India, but in 1947 he was able to return to Broadlands briefly to play host to Princess Elizabeth and the Duke of Edinburgh, who spent part of their honeymoon there. Lord Mountbatten was Prince Philip's uncle and had played an important part in his upbringing. Ten years later, as Queen, Elizabeth came to the town on an official visit for the Charter Celebrations to mark the 350th anniversary of the granting of the borough status to the town. Apart from all the official pomp and ceremony, the event is immortalised in the town's folk memory by the joker who painted footsteps from Lord Palmerston's statue to the gentlemen's convenience under the Town Hall before the Queen's visit. These were very quickly painted over, but the Queen and Prince Philip had already heard about Lord Palmerston's descent from his pedestal and were anxious to locate his footsteps.

Lord Louis Mountbatten was created Earl Mountbatten of Burma in 1948 and became First Sea Lord in 1955. From 1959 to 1965 he was Chief of the Defence Staff, the first holder of this joint post. Lady Mountbatten died in 1960 while on a tour of the Far East. She was much missed, for despite all her commitments in Asia, she still found time to attend modest town functions in Romsey. After her death her body lay in state in Romsey Abbey, prior to burial at sea. Edwina Mountbatten House, sheltered accommodation for the elderly is a lasting memorial to her. This complex, built in the style of traditional almshouses, with an elegant clock tower, is close to the gates of Broadlands.

Lord Mountbatten retired from active service in 1965 but his distinguished military career, his royal blood and his Irish estates made

Dukes Mill Shopping Complex, built on the site of the old Town Mill.

him a target for the IRA. He, with three others, was killed by a bomb in Ireland in 1979. After a State Funeral service in London, his body was brought to Romsey for burial in the Abbey. The schools and shops closed for the day and virtually every shop put black goods and mourning ribbons in the window. After the funeral, the flowers were laid out on the North Garth of the Abbey and thousands of people went to see them. There were so many flowers that even close together they covered a substantial area and they ranged from formal government tributes to modest bunches of flowers.

Since Lord Mountbatten had no son he was granted the privilege of passing the peerage to his elder daughter, Lady Brabourne, who is now Countess Mountbatten of Burma. Under her mother's will the property passed to her eldest son (although her father had had a life interest in it). After his grandfather's death, he assumed the courtesy title of Lord Romsey and took up residence at Broadlands.

Two months after Lord Mountbatten's death, the Royal family were back in Romsey for Lord Romsey's wedding. Again shops and schools were closed, but this time the windows were decorated with white and Lord Palmerston's statue sported a top hat and a buttonhole. Two years later Prince Charles brought his bride, Lady Diana Spencer, to spend part of their honeymoon at Broadlands. Quite properly, after their journey from the railway station to the house, the town saw no more of them, but saw plenty of press corps which camped outside the gates of Broadlands.

Until 1978 Broadlands was a private residence only, but in that year the Mountbatten family opened it to the public while still making it their home, and they have done so each summer since. The house is currently one of the most popular Stately Homes in England, with thousands of tourists visiting it. A sizeable number of those tourists come into Romsey to see the Abbey and the town. Their interest (and their money) is welcomed but their vehicles aggravate a difficult parking situation which has yet to be resolved. The trade they bring has encouraged the shopkeepers to smarten their shops and the attractive practice of hanging baskets of flowers outside many premises in summer is undoubtedly a response to tourism. On the other hand, the equally attractive many coloured and delicate Christmas lighting in the town, together with the floodlighting of the Abbey is primarily a "local" enthusiasm.

Romsey is not only attractive to tourists; it is a very popular place to live. The town has a flourishing social life and the high technology firms in the area are bringing a group of lively and energetic newcomers to reinforce local clubs and societies. When the Plaza cinema stopped showing films, it spent some years as a Bingo Hall. After being empty for a while, the local amateur dramatic society decided to buy it. They have

Romsey Market Place.

Prince Charles and Lady Diana Spencer, now the Princess of Wales, with Lord Romsey during their visit to Broadlands for the opening of the Mountbatten Exhibition in 1981. (Photo: Pat Sillence.)

raised thousands of pounds to purchase and renovate the building and have converted a "white elephant" into another focus of community life.

The town still has a very successful agricultural show each September, whose roots are in the nineteenth century, and in some respect it replaces the town's ancient fairs. A tradition has developed during this century of having a town carnival. This used to be predominantly a procession and a funfair. The carnival now has events spreading out over ten days and a large number of townspeople and visitors either take part or enjoy watching.

In 1974 the town lost its Borough Council under the local government reorganisation. Romsey now has a low powered Town Council and the day-to-day administration is in the hands of the Test Valley Borough Council. This body has to cope with Romsey, Stockbridge, Andover and their hinterlands. It is not an area that has any natural coherence and there is now no direct public transport between the two main towns. Andover was not allowed to keep a Town Council because the town was too big. Romsey kept a mayor and Council and they act as a focus of discussion on matters of concern to the town. Romsey is still a small town but at the moment it is a happy and successful community. In the last two thousand years it has grown from obscure Roman origins. For several centuries it housed one of the leading Abbeys for women in England. It saw the Abbey eclipsed and the town become independent so that when the Abbey was closed by Henry VIII, Romsey continued to exist. It became a borough in 1607, was raided by soldiers in the Civil War, but recovered and flourished. In the eighteenth century it lost its traditional wool industry, but found enough substitutes to maintain its prosperity until the mid-nineteenth century. By then it was losing population and lacking in vigour but it was revived by new capital in the 1880s. This input of capital enabled Romsey to survive as a viable community through the traumas of two World Wars and a major economic depression. The post-war years have seen a large influx of population, again bringing prosperity to the town. Whether Romsey remains a happy and thriving town now depends on balancing the needs of tourists and residents, and balancing the desire to build new houses with the need to provide adequate facilities for an increased population.

That is the challenge which faces Romsey at the present time and whether it will be successfully met depends partly on the good sense of the local community and partly on much wider issues of finance and politics, for Romsey can no more escape from the pressures of the twentieth century than it could escape the pressures of earlier eras.

LTVAS Group Publications

After the Rhinoceros (A history of Romsey's Railways)	£2.50
So Drunk he must have been to Romsey (A history of Romsey's Pubs and Inns)	£1.90
When the Nuns Ruled Romsey (Medieval Romsey)	£2.40
Romsey Remembers (Personal Reminiscences of Romsey)	£1.25
Wellow That Were (The story of the village of Wellow)	£1.90
When the Mammoth Roamed Romsey (A Study of the Prehistory of Romsey and District)	£2.00
Old Romsey at Work (A history of Industry and Transport)	£2.40
Sir W.P. of Romsey (SIR William Petty, 17th century polymath-colleague of Samuel Pepys)	£2.95
Romsey Schools 900 until 1940 (The story of the education of Romsey's children)	£3.50
A Slice of Old Romsey Drawing the Map of Romsey A Tour of Old Romsey	) out of print but) available) Romsey Library

The LTVAS Group was founded in 1973 with the objects of excavating sites of archaelogical interest; fostering practical interest in, and appreciation of archaeology; recording and surveying the area as existing from the archaeological viewpoint; and researching, collecting and publishing historical records of the Lower Test Valley.

The publications are available from LTVAS Group, c/o Mrs P. Genge, 3 Linden Road, Romsey SO51 8DA.

Index